Hugo Chavez

LEADER OF VENEZUELA

Hugo Chavez

LEADER OF VENEZUELA

Jeff C. Young

MORGAN REYNOLDS
PUBLISHING

Greensboro, North Carolina

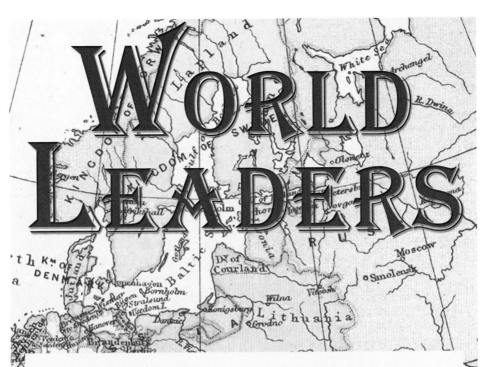

WORLD LEADERS

GEORGE C. MARSHALL
ADOLF HITLER
WOODROW WILSON
VACLAV HAVEL
GENGHIS KHAN
JOSEPH STALIN
CHE GUEVARA
FIDEL CASTRO
HUGO CHAVEZ

HUGO CHAVEZ: LEADER OF VENEZUELA

Copyright © 2007 by Jeff C. Young

Young, Jeff C., 1948-
  Hugo Chavez : leader of Venezuela / by Jeff C. Young. -- 1st ed.
    p. cm.
  Includes bibliographical references and index.
  ISBN-13: 978-1-59935-068-4
  ISBN-10: 1-59935-068-8
  1. Chavez Frmas, Hugo. 2. Venezuela--History--1974-1999. 3. Venezuela-
-History--1999- 4. Presidents--Venezuela--Biography. I. Title.
  F2329.22.C54Y68 2007
  987.06'42092--dc22
  [B]

                                             2007016946

Printed in the United States of America
First Edition

To my Aunt, Mary Beth Hanna (1921–2005),
for steadfastly believing in me.

Contents

Hugo Chavez
(AP Images/Leslie Mazoch)

one
Oil and Baseball

I n 1992, after the arrest of Venezuelan military officer Hugo Chavez, the Spanish phrase *por ahora*, which translates into English as "for the moment," began to appear spray painted on bridges and buildings throughout the country. In time, this slogan would help to change the government of Latin America's most oil rich country, and it would transform Hugo Chavez from political prisoner to head of state.

From the beginning of his career as the leader of Venezuela, Chavez has continued to worry many world leaders. His control of vast reserves of oil, a vital and dwindling resource, makes it impossible to ignore him. Furthermore, Chavez has aggressively antagonized the United States and has sought to build alliances with Cuba, Iran, and Syria—three nations that are avowed enemies of the United States.

Chavez called U.S. President George W. Bush "an illegitimate president" and "the result of a fraud" because of the controversial election in 2000. In September 2006, in

An oil refinery in Venezuela *(AP Images/ Sincor/HO)*

an address to the United Nations, Chavez called Bush "the devil" and accused him of "talking as if he owned the world." During his impassioned twenty-three minute speech, the Venezuelan president also called the American president "a spokesman of imperialism" who was trying "to preserve the current pattern of domination, exploitation, and pillage of the peoples of the world."

Yet despite these tensions, the U.S. and Venezuela continue to do business with one another. Venezuela needs the revenue that comes from selling oil to the United States, and the U.S. needs the oil. In 2005, around 11 percent of America's imported oil came from Venezuela and more than 50 percent of Venezuela's exported oil went to the America. Only Canada, Mexico and Saudi Arabia export more oil to the U.S.

If a major war in the Middle East reduced Saudi Arabia's oil exports to America, Venezuela could become even more vital to America's economic well being. According to a 2004 estimate, Venezuela had oil reserves of 77.8 billion barrels; the U.S. has 22 billion. Venezuela also has an estimated 260 billion barrels of heavy, crude oil in the center of the country. Some analysts say that by 2020, Venezuela will pass Mexico as an oil importer to the United States.

Even before he was elected president, Chavez viewed oil as a potent weapon for influencing other nations. "Oil is a geopolitical weapon," he declared, "and the imbeciles who govern us don't realize the power they have as an oil-producing country."

Hugo Chavez has made himself into a formidable figure in international politics, one who will not be ignored. To understand what motivates him, it is necessary to look at the forces that changed him from a loyal military officer into a revolutionary.

In upbringing, education, and family wealth, Chavez enjoyed a better life than most Venezuelans. However, that doesn't mean that he enjoyed an easy life.

Hugo Chavez was born on July 28, 1954, in Sabaneta, Venezuela, the second of six children born to elementary school teachers, Hugo de los Reyes Chavez and Elena Frias. Chavez grew up in a modest riverside house with mud floors and a palm roof.

Both of Hugo's parents were politically active. His father worked as a political organizer and was elected governor of the state of Barinas after he retired from teaching.

Hugo's parents were the latest in a line of revolutionary fighters: his great-grandfather, Colonel Pedro Perez Perez,

In this photograph, Chavez stands with his father, Hugo de los Reyes Chavez. (*AP Images/Andres Leighton*)

was a guerilla who fought the powerful landowners who ruled Venezuela in the 1840s. Hugo's grandfather, General Pedro Perez Delgado, fought to overthrow the dictatorship of General Juan Vicente Gomez early in the twentieth century, but died in prison after being captured by General Gomez's soldiers. Chavez's grandmother would tell young Hugo stories of how soldiers had burned down their barn and all the buildings on their family farm.

As the son of educators, Chavez was given a love of reading and learning. He was an outstanding student and an avid reader and graduated near the top of his high school class.

Chavez credits his parents with emphasizing the importance of studying and seeing that their children got the best education they could. "They inculcated to us the importance of studies," he told journalist Ted Koppel. "But out of every one hundred children from my town, ninety-nine didn't get to study. That was poverty, the poorest of farmers."

Despite this focus on education, Hugo's main interest was baseball. In other Latin American countries, soccer is the most popular sport, but in Venezuela baseball has been the most popular sport since it was introduced there in the 1890s. The country has produced several major league stars, including Hall of Fame shortstop Luis Aparicio and the more recent stars Omar Vizquel, Magglio Ordonez, and Bobby Abreu. For many years, major and minor league players from the United States have played in the winter baseball leagues in Venezuela to sharpen their skills during the off-season.

Hugo longed to be a major league pitcher: "One of my greatest dreams was to be a pitcher for the San Francisco Giants. I played a lot of baseball. It was a passion of mine."

After finishing high school, Chavez enrolled in the tuition-free Venezuelan Military Academy. The school was well known for both its strong academic program and its baseball teams. It gave Chavez the chance to get an education and pursue his dream of someday playing major league baseball. "The army for me was the only way to the major leagues," Chavez told an interviewer. "My father could not pay for my studies anywhere else."

As a young man, Hugo played for a national team called *Criollitos de Venezuela*. He continued to excel at the sport as an adult while playing for teams affiliated with educational or military institutions.

In his formative years, Chavez's main interest was playing baseball. This 2003 photo shows Chavez throwing a pitch for the Venezuelan team during an exhibition game with Cuba. *(AP Images/Leslie Mazoch)*

But when an arm injury abruptly ended Hugo's dreams of baseball stardom, he turned his attention and energies toward becoming a career soldier. He graduated from the Military Academy in 1975 and joined an elite unit of paratroopers. Chavez ascended to the rank of lieutenant colonel, but he became increasingly concerned about the effectiveness and integrity of the government that he was serving.

Throughout its history, Venezuela has been ruled by repressive governments. Spain exercised colonial control for centuries after Columbus set foot on the South American mainland in 1498. In the 1500s, Spain established settlements in Venezuela. Many of Venezuela's native Indian population were forced by the Spanish settlers to become slaves on their large coffee and sugar plantations known as haciendas. Others were captured and branded by the Spaniards, then sold to work as slaves on various Caribbean islands.

The ruthless exploitation of South American Indians caused a huge drop in their numbers. In the 1400s, South America was home to an estimated population of 50 million Indians. By the end of the Spanish Conquest, a mere 2 million remained. That led to a large importation of African slaves from the islands of the Caribbean.

In spite of exploiting the native populace and such natural resources as pearls, cacao (seeds used to make chocolate), sugar, and coffee, it cost Spain more to govern and occupy Venezuela than it collected in taxes and exports. But Spain needed Venezuela because Portugal, the Netherlands, and England all had nearby colonies. Those three countries were all looking to expand their land holdings and political control in South America and in the Caribbean, and Spain's occupation of Venezuela served as a deterrent to their expansionist plans.

During the 1600s, agriculture was Venezuela's major economic activity. Wheat, tobacco, and cotton were major exports. The prominent trade city Caracas became the country's political, economic, and cultural center. The increased trade gave rise to the formation of the Caracas Company in 1728. That same year, Spain gave the Caracas Company a monopoly on all trade within Venezuela.

The Caracas Company controlled the nation's economy for about fifty years. Exports to Spain increased, but wages for Venezuelan workers stayed low and the prices for imported goods stayed high.

By the late eighteenth century, an independence movement was emerging. In 1795, slaves and free laborers joined forces to seize control of several plantations before being subdued by the Spanish forces. Eleven years later, Francisco de Miranda tried to liberate Venezuela from Spanish rule. Known as *El*

Precursor (the Forerunner), Miranda was born in Caracas and had fought in the American Revolution. Miranda raised a volunteer army of around two hundred soldiers to liberate Venezuela.

His invasion failed to attract additional support for his cause, though. Miranda retreated to London but later returned to again lead rebel forces. In 1812, he surrendered to the Spanish forces. His Spanish captors ignored the terms of his surrender and deported Miranda to Spain as a political prisoner, where he died in prison in 1816.

The independence movement begun by Miranda was continued by Simon Bolivar.

Bolivar had served as an aide to Miranda. In 1813, he led a successful military campaign that temporarily freed Venezuela from Spanish rule and earned him the title of "Liberator."

In 1806, Francisco de Miranda led a failed attempt to liberate Venezuela from Spanish control.

Chavez speaks in front of a large portrait of Simon Bolivar. *(AP Images/Juan Carlos Solorzano, Miraflores)*

When Spanish forces regained control of Venezuela, Bolivar fled to Haiti, where he found the financial backing to lead another insurrection against the Spanish.

After combining his forces with the soldiers led by patriot leader Jose Antonio Paez, Bolivar began freeing Venezuela and the neighboring nation of Nueva Granada (New Granada) from Spanish rule. Bolivar went on to liberate what are now the nations of Venezuela, Ecuador, Colombia, and Panama.

Bolivar had a grand scheme for uniting the liberated countries. In 1819, Colombia and Venezuela united to form a republic called Gran Colombia. Two years later, Panama joined the republic, and in 1822, Ecuador joined. Bolivar served as president of Gran Colombia while continuing to lead military campaigns against the Spanish. By 1825, he had become the most powerful man in South America.

Internal political squabbles in Gran Colombia finally forced Bolivar to assume dictatorial powers. This led to an assassination attempt and ultimately to Bolivar resigning as president in 1830. Still, Bolivar is today revered by Venezuelans much as Americans revere George Washington—as a military leader and revolutionary who freed his country from foreign rule.

From 1830 to 1935, Venezuela was ruled by a series of military dictators known as caudillos. The caudillos exercised complete control of the government. They refused to share power with the legislature or the courts.

One of the most notorious of the caudillos was General Juan Vicente Gomez, who ruled Venezuela from 1908 to 1935. Gomez abolished all rival political parties and used the military and his secret police to crush dissent. Thousands of people were tortured, imprisoned, or forced to leave Venezuela during his brutal rule.

Gomez was ruthless and corrupt but his reign was relatively prosperous thanks to the country's emergence as a major oil producing nation. Rich deposits of oil had been found around Lake Maracaibo in northern Venezuela. Indians had used the gooey black substance to waterproof their canoes. Spanish explorers noticed the presence of oil, but they were much more interested in gold. But after automobiles and trucks became a major means of transportation in the early twentieth century, the worldwide demand for oil greatly increased.

In 1922, the Royal Dutch Shell Company found a huge deposit of oil on the northeastern shore of Lake Maracaibo. The area was called the Bolivar Field and is the third-largest oil field in the world, and the largest outside of the Middle East.

Before long, it was producing more than 100,000 barrels of oil a day. By 1928, Venezuela was the world's leading exporter of oil.

The oil boom forever changed the economy and importance of Venezuela. Venezuelans abandoned their traditional jobs in agriculture, ranching, and manufacturing to work in the oil industry. The infusion of oil money, or "petrodollars" as it came to be called, gave rise to a growing urban middle class and increased government spending for education, social services, and infrastructure.

Gomez used some of the revenues from oil exports to build roads, railroads, and upgrade ports, but he kept much of the petrodollars for his own use. During Gomez's reign, most Venezuelans still lived impoverished lives. When he died in 1938, Gomez was one of the wealthiest men in Venezuela.

Between 1935 and 1958, Venezuela moved back and forth between civilian and military rule. A few political reforms were instituted. Labor unions and opposition political parties were allowed to openly operate. Welfare benefit programs aided the country's poorest citizens.

When Chavez was born in 1954, Venezuela was ruled by one of its most repressive and ruthless dictators, Marcos Perez Jimenez. Jimenez established a network of police and informants to spy on, harass, intimidate, and imprison anyone who dared to oppose him. While he was in power, Jimenez plundered the nation's resources for personal gain. When he was forced out of office in 1958, his net worth was an estimated $700 million.

The end of Jimenez's reign ushered in an era of democratic rule and free elections. Jimenez had outlawed political parties but after his removal three major political parties returned—the liberal Democratic Action (AD), the conservative COPEI (Committee of Independent Electoral Political Organization) and the URD (Democratic Republican Union).

In 1958, leaders of the three parties met at Punto Fijo and signed an agreement to share power. The agreement ensured that the party in power would appoint members of the opposition parties to cabinet and government ministry positions. When the URD withdrew from the agreement, the AD and COPEI parties became Venezuela's two dominant parties.

Until the 1990s, Venezuela was controlled by a two-party system, though there were some sporadic attempts by guerrillas to disrupt elections by threats, kidnappings, and violence. A coalition of rebels and political groups who called themselves the Armed Forces of National Liberation (FALN) enjoyed the support of Cuban leader Fidel Castro. They hoped to topple the government by recruiting members of Venezuela's rural poor to their cause. FALN was never able to garner widespread popular support and in 1967 the Communist Party withdrew their support of the rebel group. Two years later, Venezuela legalized FALN as a political party.

Fluctuating oil prices, large-scale corruption, and the distribution of oil revenues were more vexing problems than FALN. In the 1970s, Venezuela's oil income quadrupled. At that time, Carlos Andres Perez was serving as president. He embarked on a huge spending spree to spread the vast oil wealth to all the people.

When Perez was inaugurated as president, Chavez was nineteen and attended the ceremony. The pomp and pageantry of the event made an indelible impression on him. He wrote in his diary: "Watching him pass, I imagined myself walking there with the weight of the country on my own shoulders."

During his first term as president (1974-79), Perez worked at creating jobs and increasing economic opportunities for all Venezuelans, but most of the nation's wealth remained in the hands of the middle and upper classes. Perez also brought the nation's petroleum, oil, and steel industries under government control, greatly increasing Venezuela's control of the revenues generated by those industries. Then, in 1983, oil prices plummeted and drastic cuts had to be made in the social welfare programs Perez had initiated. Those spending cuts led to some violent demonstrations and rioting.

In 1988, Perez was once again elected president. Shortly after beginning his second term, economic conditions forced him to raise the prices on gasoline and public transportation. The continuing decline of oil prices and pervasive government corruption had depleted the national treasury. Venezuela also owed a huge debt to other nations and foreign banks. Perez was forced to raise taxes and reduce spending on social welfare.

Perez's second term ended when the Venezuelan legislature forced him out of office in May 1993. He was impeached on corruption charges and placed under house arrest.

During this time, Chavez was torn between devotion to duty as a military officer and disgust and dissatisfaction with a succession of ineffective and corrupt governments. Most of his countrymen still lived in abject poverty and the gap between rich and poor steadily increased. Chavez knew that making major changes would entail taking major risks. Yet, he was ready to assume those risks. He was ready to lead if he could find enough followers.

two
Young Revolutionary

I n 1974, when he was a twenty-year-old academy cadet, Hugo Chavez visited Peru with a dozen fellow soldiers. They had traveled there to help celebrate the one-hundred-fiftieth anniversary of the Battle of Ayacucho. The trip would prove to be a key event in his life.

The 1824 battle marked the liberation of Peru from Spanish rule; the liberating forces had been led by Simon Bolivar. Chavez had grown up hearing and reading tales of how Bolivar had also freed Venezuela from Spanish rule and tried to unite the liberated South American countries into one nation.

When Chavez went to Peru, the country was ruled by a military regime. But it was a type of military rule different than anything he had experienced in Venezuela. In 1968, General Juan Velasco Alvarado seized power and became Peru's new head of state. However, unlike most South American military dictators, who were usually supported by the right-wing

Former Venezuelan president Carlos Andres Perez *(AP Images/Ricardo Mazalan)*

officers and wealthy conservatives that resisted social reform and redistribution of wealth, Alvarado enjoyed the support of both the military and members of Peru's left-wing parties.

Alvarado instituted a program of reforms that created farm cooperatives from what were once large estates, and implemented a series of measures to protect workers and attempted to redistribute income and wealth. His administration also nationalized many industries, helping to ensure that the government would have more revenue for financing his reforms.

The trip to Peru made a lasting impression on Chavez. He saw that it was possible to have a government that was ruled by a strong military leader that was also dedicated to reform and increased and improved economic opportunities for its poorest citizens.

A year after his visit to Peru, Chavez graduated from the military academy. During the graduation ceremonies, Venezuelan President Carlos Andres Perez handed out swords to Chavez and the other graduates. It was an impressive symbolic ritual, almost an omen of future events. In February 1992, Chavez and some of his classmates would try to overthrow Perez's government.

For the first two years after his graduation, Chavez was stationed with a battalion fighting leftist guerillas inside Venezuela. According to Chavez, his political sympathies shifted from supporting General Perez to siding with the guerillas. Chavez also began to see how political corruption was affecting the military. He watched officers submit false budget requests and steal equipment for their personal use.

By 1977, Chavez formed a small armed group called the *Ejercito de Liberacion del Pueblo de Venezuela* (ELPV), the Liberation Army of the Venezuelan People, within the army. Years later, Chavez was asked about the purpose of the ELPV. He candidly acknowledged that they didn't have one at that time. They wanted to be ready just in case General Perez was removed from power. "We did it to prepare ourselves in case something should happen," Chavez said. "We hadn't the least idea at that time what we were going to do."

In 1980, Chavez left active duty to return to the military academy in Caracas as a member of its faculty. Initially, he returned to pursuing his baseball interests as the academy's chief sports instructor. Then he served as a tutor in history and politics. He was regarded as an intelligent, articulate, and influential instructor and mentor to the cadets.

Chavez worked at the academy until 1985. During that time, he became convinced that the military would be called upon to remove General Perez and establish a new government.

The 1970s had been a time of immense prosperity as petro-dollars flowed into Venezuela. Yet, little of the money went to help the nation's poorest and neediest. In the 1980s, after the drastic decrease in oil prices, it was revealed that Venezuela didn't have an economy diversified enough to withstand the huge drop in revenue. There was a sharp rise in unemployment and less money available to help the unemployed.

By 1982, Chavez believed that he needed to organize a revolutionary movement to take over the government. He recruited two fellow officers and academy lecturers to form a movement called the *Movimiento Bolivariano Revolucionario-200* (MBR-200) or Bolivarian Revolutionary Movement. The "200" was added because 1983 would mark the 200th anniversary of Bolivar's birth.

On December 17, 1982, Chavez met with his fellow revolutionaries. In a solemn ceremony, they repeated the pledge Simon Bolivar had made when he devoted his life to freeing Venezuela from Spanish rule: "I swear before you, and I swear before the God of my fathers, that I will not allow my arm to relax nor my soul to rest until I have broken the chains that oppress us."

At first, MBR-200 was more of a political study group than a circle of revolutionary conspirators. But as they studied Venezuela's history and current problems, they began believing that a coup was the proper way to affect change.

In a 1999 interview, Chavez explained why he had lost confidence in the existing government and political system in 1982:

> What has been called the democratic system in Venezuela has not differed much in recent years from what came before: the dictatorship of Marcos Perez Jiminez; the three years of government [of *Accion Democratica*] between 1945 and 1948; the governments of Isaias Medina and Lopez Contreras; and even the government of Juan Vicente Gomez, which takes us back to 1908. Everything has basically remained the same; it's been the same system of domination, with a different face—whether it's that of General Gomez or of Doctor Rafael Caldera. Behind this figure, this caudillo with a military beret or without it, on horseback or in a Cadillac or a Mercedes Benz, it's been the same system—in economics and in politics—and the same denial of basic human rights and of the right of the people to determine their own destiny.

Working and lecturing at the military academy put Chavez and his friends in a perfect position to recruit like-minded military officers and academy cadets to their cause. Throughout

Caracas, Venezuela's capital city

the 1980s, members of MBR-200 were content to bide their time. But while they were patiently waiting, Venezuela's military intelligence agency was keeping a watchful eye on them.

The *Direccion de Inteligencia Military* (DIM) knew that Chavez and other academy lecturers were espousing radical revolutionary ideas in their lectures. What they didn't know was how widespread the MBR-200 had become. The officers in the movement were some of the nation's most promising, popular, and able military leaders. Any attempts to silence or discipline them would be widely unpopular with other soldiers and officers.

The people in power decided that the best solution was to remove Chavez from the academy and to send him far away from Caracas, the nation's capital. He was shunted off to a post near the Colombian border, Elorza in the region of Apure.

Chavez organized historical pageants and encouraged the natives to begin oral history projects. These outreaches made him a popular and prominent figure in the region of Apure. Ever the politician, he was quietly building a base of supporters.

By 1988, the leaders in Caracas had either forgiven or forgotten Chavez's past transgressions. He was brought back to Caracas to work as an aide to the national security council. At Elorza, Chavez had been effectively isolated from his fellow officers in the MBR-200. Now he was in a position to further his conspiratorial plans to overthrow the government.

Chavez had long hoped for a spark to ignite the fires of a revolution. But when that spark occurred, Chavez and his fellow members of the MBR-200 were woefully unprepared to lead an insurrection.

It began in the town of Guarenas, located about twenty miles east of Caracas. Many residents used the local bus lines to commute to jobs in Caracas. On the morning of February 27, 1989, the commuting workers found that the bus fare had doubled overnight. Before the overnight increase, students were entitled to a half-price bus fare, but this also was changed. Low-paid workers and students dependent on public transportation were suddenly unable to live within their budgets. Soon, there were protests throughout the town. By midmorning, the protests had spread to some of Venezuela's major cities. Buses were overturned and burned, and that was just the beginning.

Within a few hours, there was widespread looting and the destruction of stores and shops. In Caracas, gangs of angry youths rioted and looted throughout the night. This spontaneous rebellion came to be known as the Caracazo.

But while the Caracazo was gaining momentum and popular support, Chavez was bedridden with a contagious illness, and had been sent home to prevent him from infecting his co-workers at the presidential palace. Officers who had secretly sworn alliance to the MBR-200 were forced to repress an uprising they had long waited to happen. Chavez would later tell an interviewer that he would not have fired at civilians, even if he had been ordered to.

> I was a simple soldier then. Just a soldier with a good future and everything going along well, but then I had to ask, "What do I do with this rifle, where do I point it?" It was a terrible crisis of conscience. Now that the hurricane is unleashed, what do I do? Do I throw my rifle on the ground and run off, and

On the third day of the 1989 riots, Perez was forced to order the Venezuelan military to curb the riots and looting. *(AP Images/John Hooper)*

stop being a soldier, or do I point it at miserable peasants? Or do I point it against those who have lead the people to this situation? My comrades and I took the road of Bolivar, who said, "Damned be the soldier who turns his weapons against his people."

Like Chavez and the MBR-200 supporters, the government of incumbent President Carlos Andres Perez was unprepared for the sudden uprising. In mid-February, Perez had announced increased prices on gasoline and public transportation. He had anticipated a gradual fare increase by the bus owners, but he didn't order them to implement one. The sudden 100 percent increase took everyone by surprise.

During the first two days of rioting, the police didn't intervene. On the third day, the National Guard was called in but they also refused to get involved. This forced Perez to use the military to brutally suppress the widespread rioting and looting.

Soldiers were given free reign to shoot looters and anyone else who disobeyed their orders to disperse. The government claimed that 372 people were killed, but another estimate claimed that there were over 2,000 casualties just in Caracas. Thousands more were wounded.

While his illness prevented Chavez from seizing the opportunity to lead a rebellion, it may have saved his life. One of his closest associates, Felipe Acosta Carles, was killed while subduing some rioters. The exact circumstances of his death remain a mystery. Chavez believes that the secret police, aware of Carles's involvement with the MBR-200, had him killed and blamed his death on the rioters.

Even though he was bedridden during the short-lived Caracazo, soldiers were still looking to Chavez to lead some kind of coup. When he returned to his duties at the presidential palace, members of the elite palace guard asked him about the MBR-200. One of the guard members pointedly asked him: "Look here Major, is it true about the Bolivarian Movement? We'd like to hear more about it; we're not prepared to go on killing people."

His question validated what Chavez had come to believe: if soldiers who were entrusted with protecting the president expressed interest in the MBR-200, there must be widespread dissatisfaction with the ruling regime.

But the members of the palace guard weren't the only soldiers interested in the MBR-200. The nation's highest ranking officers had become suspicious of Chavez. In December 1989, Chavez and several other majors were ordered to appear before the army high command. They were all accused of conspiring against the government and plotting to assassinate President Perez and other high ranking officers. All the evidence against them was hearsay—they could not definitively prove the existence of an ongoing conspiracy.

Without solid evidence, the only thing the high command could do was separate the majors by sending them to remote outposts throughout the country. Chavez was granted permission to enroll at Simon Bolivar University in Caracas to pursue a master's degree in political science. The coup was postponed.

But by August 1991, the situation had changed again. Chavez had completed his studies and was assigned to lead a battalion of paratroopers. How and why the wily Chavez had regained the trust of the military leaders remains a mystery. Regardless, he had soldiers at his command—and was ready to resume the work of the MBR-200.

three
Coming to Power

I n December 1991, Chavez was given command of a regiment of paratroopers stationed in Maracay, about fifty miles southwest of Caracas. While serving there, he plotted the overthrow of President Perez. Initially, he planned to stage a coup the same month that he assumed command of the regiment, but changed his plans after news of the impending coup was leaked. The identity of the informant or informants remains a mystery, but it was probably one or more of the civilian collaborators he had trusted.

A new plan was soon cooked up, however. The coup was scheduled to begin on February 4, 1992, when President Perez was scheduled to return to Venezuela from a trip abroad. The plan was to seize President Perez at the airport. Chavez calculated that about 10 percent of the Venezuelan military was on his side. But if the coup were to succeed, President Perez would have to be captured in the first few hours. If the president remained free to command the military, the coup would be quashed.

According to Chavez, plans were finalized after informants inside the presidential palace told him exactly when President Perez would be returning. He recalled,

> We had been on the alert since Thursday, January 30. A final meeting had been held on Sunday, at a petrol (gasoline) station on the Pan-American highway, with the Bolivarian conspirators in the air force . . . I remember that on Sunday, February 2, almost at midnight, our people rang me from Miraflores Palace and told me, in code, the date and time of the return of Perez. That was the moment that we began to activate the operation, and on the Monday we woke up and started getting people on the move.

Although Chavez and his conspirators knew when and where President Perez would be returning, their coup was doomed. At around noon on Monday, February 4, a captain they trusted betrayed them. The captain was stationed at the military academy in Caracas and had been entrusted to capture and detain the academy's senior officers. Instead, he told the academy director that a coup was imminent.

By the evening of February 3, the first stages of the coup were underway. Military installations at Maracay, Maracaibo, and other cities were already under the control of the conspirators. The next step was to advance on Caracas and seize control of the capital. But telephone calls made to other military bases revealed that things were awry. Using an easily understood code, the conspirators acknowledged things weren't going according to plan.

"I can't make it."

"The party's today, send me the whiskey."

"No we can't send the whiskey, we couldn't get the money."

"OK, don't send me anything."

While the coup was floundering, Chavez gamely proceeded with his plan to capture Caracas. On Sunday evening, a caravan of rented buses left Maracay for Caracas. Chavez had planned to station his soldiers inside the city's Historical Museum and make it their command center. When they arrived at the museum, they were met with machine gunfire.

Chavez realized that he had been betrayed but refused to surrender. He brazenly talked his way into the museum by claiming that he and his men were there as reinforcements. When he got inside he expected to find phones he could use to communicate with his soldiers. No phones were available, though. His coup was coming apart.

In Caracas, the rebels attacked the presidential palace but were unable to storm the building. Their reinforcements were rebuffed when they tried to enter the capital city. Air force generals who had sworn their support to the coup lost their nerve and grounded their planes, leaving the rebels with no air cover. The civilians who were supposed to take over the radio and television stations failed to fulfill their mission. Chavez later recalled:

> The civilians didn't show up. I had a lorry (truck) near Miraflores filled with guns to be handed out to civilians. Although it's true that we didn't control the media, and we were unable to appeal for popular support, it's also true that there were people who knew that that was the night of the operation. . . . But they didn't show up. We are not the only ones to blame. There were people who had known about the operation in advance, and they simply didn't come.

President Perez made a nationwide televised address, announcing that a military rebellion that had begun in Maracay was being crushed. Chavez watched the broadcast and soon afterward decided to surrender and throw himself at the mercy of the government he had tried to overthrow. He claimed that he surrendered to avoid more bloodshed.

After surrendering, Chavez asked for permission to speak on television and the government agreed. This decision to allow Chavez television time would ultimately lead to his taking power in Venezuela. Although his speech lasted for less than a minute, it was long enough for Chavez to go from being an obscure colonel who had led a failed coup to a dynamic and charismatic political leader.

Clad in his army uniform and paratrooper's red beret, Chavez looked into the television camera and praised his soldiers for their courage. Then he announced that their coup had failed, but defiantly said that there would be another time for them to fight:

> Comrades: unfortunately, for the moment, the objectives that we have set for ourselves have not been achieved in the capital. That's to say that those of us here in Caracas have not been able to seize power. Where you are, you have performed well, but now is the time for a rethink; new possibilities sill arise again and the country will be able to move definitively to a better future.
>
> So listen to what I have to say, listen to Commandant Chavez who is sending you this message, and please, think deeply. Lay down you arms, for in truth the objectives that we set ourselves at a national level are not within our grasp.
>
> Comrades, listen to this message of solidarity. I am grateful for your loyalty, your courage, and for your selfless generosity; before the country and before you, I alone shoulder the responsibility for this Bolivarian military uprising. Thank you.

Chavez is escorted by military officers after being arrested for his orchestration of a failed coup attempt. *(AP Images/Andres Leighton)*

Under most other regimes that had held power in Venezuela, Chavez could have been executed for treason. Instead, he was imprisoned with nine other coup leaders. The harsh early days of his imprisonment were a shock to him. "The first days were like being in a grave," Chavez recalled. "It was cold and we were kept in a basement. I felt as if I had been buried alive."

While the conditions of his imprisonment were harsh, Chavez eventually received some special privileges. He was

Many supporters of Chavez wear a red beret similar to the one he wore during his televised 1992 speech. *(AP Images/Esteban Felix)*

allowed to be interviewed for radio programs and received numerous visitors, many of whom would later serve in his administration.

Chavez was treated more like a military hero than a dangerous revolutionary. An open-air caged yard was built just for him. According to one prison official, Chavez would sit in the yard every morning and talk to a plaster bust of Simon Bolivar.

Like countless other prisoners, Chavez and the other coup leaders found that reading was one the best ways to pass time while imprisoned. They filled their idle hours by reading from the Bible, and the philosophical writings of Plato, Karl Marx, and French writers Albert Camus and Jean-Paul Sartre. "We started studying things like political doctrines," Chavez said,

While in prison, Chavez passed the time by reading books about social reform by philosophers such as Karl Marx. *(Library of Congress)*

"I was maintaining my physical and moral strength. We were opening ourselves up to many new ideas."

If government officials believed that imprisoning Chavez and his cohorts would force them into obscurity, they miscalculated. The people of Venezuela were coming to revere Chavez as a champion of the poor and underprivileged.

In November 1992, another coup attempted to remove Perez from power. This time the coup was led by a group of air force officers. The presidential palace was bombed from the air, while rebels and soldiers still loyal to Perez fought in the streets. There was also an armed attempt to free Chavez from prison.

The second coup attempt was bloodier than the first, with around 170 fatalities. Clearly, Venezuela's political system was starting to unravel. President Perez was losing his tenuous grip on power.

In March 1993, Perez was charged with embezzling $17 million of government funds for what was termed "nonofficial" use. He was found guilty by the Venezuelan Supreme Court and forced to resign. The Venezuelan Senate then appointed Senator Ramon Jose Velasquez to finish out the last eight months of Perez's term.

Another presidential election was held in December 1993. Chavez urged his supporters to boycott the election and an estimated 40 percent of the electorate abstained from voting. Four candidates ran and a former president, Rafael Caldera, was elected with just 30 percent of the vote. The country's two main parties, COPEI and Democratic Action, were out of power for the first time in thirty-five years.

Caldera realized that Chavez's call for a boycott helped to get him elected. As a reward, he pardoned Chavez. On March 27, 1994, Colonel Chavez became a free man.

Normally, an ex-prisoner, especially one who tried to overthrow a government, would be barred from seeking political office. But for Chavez there was an incredible loophole. Although he had been jailed for nearly two years, Chavez had never been officially sentenced. Therefore, he was eligible to run for office. He soon formed a new party that he called the *Movimiento Quinta Repubilica* (Fifth Republic Movement or MVR).

While insisting that he wasn't a candidate for any office, Chavez barnstormed his way through Venezuela, making speeches calling for the dissolution of the National Assembly. A 1994 article in the *Washington Post* made note of Chavez's growing popularity:

> Chavez has become kind of a cult figure whose strident rhetoric—advocating stern anti-corruption moves and selected uncompensated seizure of private property—is finding an audience. With the financial system of this historically wealthy oil-exporting nation in virtual collapse, its economic prospects clouded and its politicians discredited by scandals, many Venezuelans are looking for a savior. Chavez offers himself for the role.

Although Chavez was again immersed in politics, that wasn't his only interest. While he was imprisoned, Chavez's first wife divorced him. It didn't take him long to remarry. While giving speeches in late 1996, he met a newspaper columnist named Marisabel. She passed a note to Chavez and a love affair quickly began. The couple had a daughter, Rosines, and in December 1997, three months after Rosines's birth, they were wed in a private ceremony.

Some of Chavez's political detractors claim that his second marriage was politically motivated. They said that Chavez married the blue-eyed, blond Marisabel because she would make a more glamorous First Lady than his first wife. However, the marriage hasn't survived the turmoil of politics and ruling a nation. Shortly after Chavez was first elected president, she was hospitalized for stress. Later the couple separated.

Although he worked at founding and building a new political party, Chavez repeatedly denied that he was seeking any political office. A year before the presidential election of 1998 there was little popular support for him. A poll taken in December 1997 showed that less than 12 percent of likely voters said they would vote for Chavez.

Even though he seemingly had little support, there was a feeling in the country that it was time for a change. Chavez emphasized the nation's economic woes in his speeches. Venezuelans seeking loans were paying an annual percentage rate of nearly 100 percent. Banks were demanding that business owners put up their cars or houses as collateral before they could get a business loan.

Venezuela was also suffering from an overvalued currency, a falling stock market, and an overall feeling that the huge oil revenues were not benefiting the ordinary citizen.

One nationwide poll revealed that more than 85 percent of Venezuelans felt that they were cheated out of the benefits of oil wealth. That figure was very close to the number of Venezuelans said to be living in poverty, around 80 percent.

As late as spring of 1998, polls showed that Chavez was still far behind Irene Saez, a one-time winner of the Miss Universe Beauty Pageant. Saez was favored by 35.7 percent of the voters to only 20.7 percent for Chavez. However, an endorsement from one of Venezuela's two traditional parties doomed her candidacy. Saez had presented herself as an outsider to the parties that had ruled Venezuela for so long. After the endorsement, she was seen as just another part of the same system that needed to be changed and her popularity ratings fell to less than 10 percent. "What people hadn't counted on was the real depth of disgust that Venezuelans had for traditional politics," said an unnamed diplomat.

With the decline of Saez, Henrique Salas Romer emerged as Chavez's major opponent. Romer had some impressive credentials. He graduated from Yale University and had served two terms as the governor of the state of Carabobo. At his campaign rallies he appeared astride a white horse named Frijolito, or Little Bean. But like Saez, his popularity eroded because of the support of the major parties—the Democratic Action and the COPEI. In a last ditch effort to stop Chavez, both of these parties endorsed Romer.

Chavez talks with Irene Saez in this photograph. Saez, a former Miss Universe, ran against Chavez during the 1998 presidential campaign. *(AP Images/Jose Caruci)*

During his campaign, Chavez traveled to the most remote areas of the country and ran on a platform of making sweeping changes in the government. Along with calling for a new constitution, Chavez said that he would dissolve the National Assembly. His pledges to end corruption and spread the immense oil wealth to the poorest citizens had a strong appeal to voters who had felt neglected and ignored.

His opponents attacked Chavez as a dangerous demagogue and a dictator in waiting. The United States sided with his opposition and even denied Chavez a visa to visit America during his campaign. The U.S. State Department cited his involvement in the 1992 coup as the reason for the denial. Chavez turned that opposition to his advantage by portraying himself as an underdog fighting the interests of the rich and powerful, while championing the cause of the poor and underprivileged.

Both Chavez and Romer criticized the traditional party politics that had governed Venezuela for the past forty years, and both were vague about their plans for fixing the country's faltering economy. At one point Chavez said that if he were elected, he would default on Venezuela's $22 billion foreign debt. Later, he said that if he were elected, he would honor the country's foreign financial obligations.

The night before the election, a confident Chavez addressed a crowd in Caracas estimated at 700,000. Many of his supporters wore red berets identical to the one Chavez had donned that evening as a member of the military special forces. "We're witnessing a real revolution, which cannot be stopped by anything or anybody," Chavez declared. "We have a popular avalanche."

On December 6, 1998, Chavez was elected president with an impressive 56 percent of the vote. Romer received 40 percent. The once powerful AD (Democratic Action) and COPEI (Committee of Independent Electoral Political Organization) parties garnered a mere 3 percent of the vote. Chavez's win was the largest margin of victory in a Venezuelan presidential election.

The day after Chavez's election, an article in the *New York Times* expressed the growing concern that the rest of the world didn't know what to expect from president-elect Chavez. "Nobody was really sure what Venezuela would look like under Mr. Chavez, who has been called a nationalist, a Communist, a hero, and dictator manqué." The article also noted how Chavez had tailored his campaign speeches to the audience he was addressing. "His statements have ranged all over the political map, often depending on his audiences, although he has generally moved toward the center in recent weeks."

Although the U.S. Clinton Administration had denied Chavez a visa to visit the United States, after the election they hinted that he would be welcomed as a head of state. An unnamed State Department spokesman said that the earlier rejection "is in the past, and in the future we will deal with at that time."

The U.S. media further noted that Chavez had been conciliatory in his victory speech. The prevailing attitude was cautious. A *New York Times* editorial opined:

> Mr. Chavez's speeches are more conciliatory, but he still frightens Venezuela's elite and makes Washington nervous about the future of a country that is now the United States' primary source of oil. Mr. Chavez could become a populist despot,

> or could use his mandate to make long needed changes while respecting the rule of law. . . . Washington should make it clear that it will help Mr. Chavez if he respects Venezuelan's rights and the rule of law.

An article in the international edition of *Time* magazine lauded Chavez as: "the only candidate heroic enough—and ruthless enough to tear down what Venezuelans view as a hopelessly rotten system." Then, the article addressed whether Chavez was just a dictator in waiting. "But the bigger question is whether he'll fulfill his even more heroic promise: to replace Venezuela's old, jaded order with functioning democratic institutions—and not just with the rule of Hugo Chavez."

In February 1999, Chavez was sworn into office as president. Only seven years earlier he had been arrested for leading a failed coup. The new president inherited immense economic and social problems requiring almost immediate attention. High unemployment and inflation, along with a large national debt, were suffocating the nation's economy. Chavez had won the attention of the people of Venezuela, but now he ran the risk of his rhetoric colliding with economic realities. It was time to produce, time to lead.

four
Consolidating His Power

H ugo Chavez became the president of Venezuela on February 2, 1999. On his first day in power he clearly stated the immediate goals of his administration: the constitution of 1961 would be rewritten and the armed forces would take a greater role in Venezuela's economic and social life.

Early in his presidency, Chavez promised that his political philosophy couldn't be easily labeled or defined. "If you try to assess me by traditional canons of analysis, you never emerge from the confusion," he said in an April 1999 interview. "If you are attempting to determine if Chavez is of the left, right, or center, if he is a socialist, Communist or capitalist, well, I am none of those, but I have a bit of all of those."

When he assumed power there was a widespread belief that Chavez would become just another in a long line of caudillos. He eased those fears by holding numerous elections. He was determined to show the world that he would not act without the consent of the governed.

Within two weeks of taking the oath of office, Chavez issued a decree for a referendum to approve rewriting of the 1961 constitution. Chavez's political opponents saw the decree as a way for Chavez to acquire dictatorial powers, but the decree survived a legal challenge in Venezuela's Supreme Court and the referendum took place in April 1999. A reported 39 percent of Venezuela's registered voters cast ballots and an overwhelming 92 percent voted in favor of forming a new assembly to rewrite the constitution.

When elections were held to elect the members of the new assembly in July 1997, Chavez-backed candidates got 91 percent of the vote. Supporters of Chavez who ran as independents won 119 of the 131 seats in the assembly.

About a month after the new constitutional assembly was elected, an editorial in the *New York Times* cautiously noted that the assembly was overwhelmingly pro-Chavez.

> While Venezuelans overwhelmingly supported radical reform, they should be wary of the methods Mr. Chavez is using. He is drawing power into his own hands and misusing a special Constitutional Assembly meeting now in Caracas that is composed almost entirely of his supporters.

The newly elected assembly had a deadline of January 2000 for producing a new constitution but Chavez pressured them to get it done early. They held morning and afternoon sessions seven days a week and by late November 1999 they had finished their work. A new constitution was presented for a nationwide referendum that was held in December that year. Only about 45 percent of the country's registered voters

Chavez is presented with a draft of the proposed constitution by Luis Miquilena (left), president of the Constitutional Assembly. *(AP Images/Ennio Perdomo)*

cast votes in the constitutional referendum; approximately 72 percent approved the new constitution.

The new constitution centralized more power in the presidency. It gave him more power and the potential for a longer tenure in office by extending the president's term to six years and allowing him to run for reelection, after which he could run again after a ten year waiting period. Under the old constitution, the president served a single five-year term. Another significant change was the elimination of Venezuela's bicameral (two-house) legislature, replaced with a one house body called the National Assembly. There were also restrictions placed on the independence of the state oil company and public control over the military was reduced. Overall, the approval of the new constitution was a clear reaffirmation of Chavez's mandate to rule.

According to the new constitution, elections were to be held in May 2000, but problems with voting machines imported from the United States delayed the election until July. In the July elections, Chavez was once again elected president, this time with 59 percent of the vote. His supporters, sometimes known as Chavistas, who ran for the newly created National Assembly won 60 percent of the 165 seats. That was slightly less than a two-thirds majority that Chavez had hoped for, but it was a resounding victory greatly enhancing the scope and power of his presidency.

Behind the façade of elections and referendums, Chavez consolidated his power to a degree that a caudillo would envy. He began exerting control over the judiciary, the media, and the military. "There is great talk about democracy now," said Carlos Correa, a Venezuelan lawyer and human rights activist, "but in practice all decisions are concentrated in the president's hands, down to his own party's list of candidates."

Chavez's tight grip on the military made it easier for him to stay in power. Under a specially written law, he continued to serve as an active military officer. According to one estimate, one-third of Venezuela's regional governments are controlled by soldiers directly linked to Chavez. "In the past, all high-ranking promotions were reviewed by the Senate Armed Services Commission. Now, by law, they're reviewed directly by the president," Correa added.

Under the new constitution, the National Assembly appoints all judges. It has become virtually impossible to serve as a judge without the support of Chavez. He was able to get that sweeping power by promising to reform Venezuela's corrupt judicial system. In August 1999, the newly convened assembly set up a "judicial emergency commission" to evaluate the work of both the nation's individual judges and the members of the Supreme Court. The commission was

During his presidency, Chavez has maintained a close relationship with the Venezuelan military. *(AP Images/Leslie Mazoch)*

headed by Manuel Quijada, a lawyer and loyal supporter of Chavez. The commission reported that at least one-half of Venezuela's 1,200 judges were corrupt and or incompetent, and recommended they be removed from office.

The problems with the judicial system were aggravated by an explosive situation within Venezuela's prison system. There were around 23,000 people imprisoned, most of whom had never been brought to trial. On July 1, 1999, Chavez had issued a new penal code, giving accused criminals a presumption of innocence until they were convicted, and called for the guarantee of a swift trial.

The publication of the penal code gave prisoners a false hope that things were going to change. When the prisoner's situation did not change as fast as expected, riots broke out in several prisons and a dozen prisoners were killed. In a prison outside of Caracas, the National Guard had to come in with two tanks to restore order.

Further rioting was abated after the National Assembly declared a "prisons' emergency." In a radio address in early October, Chavez announced his plan for quickly using the new penal code. Teams of judges and prosecutors, along with priests and human rights activists, were sent to four of Venezuela's most dangerous prisons. Their objective was to give speedy trials to the prisoners still awaiting one. They also hoped to release many prisoners who had already served the time they would have received. Their announced goal was to clear 6,000 cases by the end of the year. They also instituted a work release program to allow prisoners to work day jobs outside of the prison walls.

The prison crisis brought further attention to reforming the judiciary. Before Chavez's presidency, Venezuelan judges were appointed by the majority party in Congress, which also chose the justices of the Supreme Court. In May 2004, Chavez was able to push a law through the National Assembly that increased the number of Supreme Court justices from twenty to thirty-two. This allowed Chavez to pack the court with handpicked justices loyal to him.

Along with increasing his power over the judiciary, Chavez expanded his control over government spending. One of his first acts as president was the passage of emergency economic measures that greatly expanded his budgetary powers. For example, it granted him the power to make fiscal decisions without the consent or consultation of the National Assembly.

Chavez followed through on an agreement made by the Caldera administration to reduce oil production and raise prices. The agreement involved Norway, Mexico, and the OPEC (Organization of Petroleum Exporting Countries) nations. By mid-1999, oil prices doubled and Venezuela's national debt was greatly reduced.

Chavez had only been in office about ten months before Venezuela suffered a catastrophic natural disaster. In mid-December 1999, torrential rains triggered a series of mudslides that killed tens of thousands of people and destroyed thousands of homes. The disaster occurred in the state of Vargas, just north of Caracas. The exact death toll is still unknown, but estimates range from a low of 10,000 to a high of 50,000. Most of the victims were buried under an avalanche of trees, rocks, and mud. An additional 100,000 to 140,000 survivors were left homeless.

Chavez's critics blamed him for ignoring the worsening weather conditions that caused the disaster. They said that he was too distracted with the upcoming referendum on the new

This aerial photo shows the destruction caused by the 1999 mudslide in the city of Vargas. *(AP Images/Ricardo Mazalan)*

constitution. Chavez responded to their criticism by saying: "They should shoot me if I have any possible responsibility in this."

While Chavez doesn't bear any personal responsibility for the horrendous disaster, he stubbornly refused most offers of aid from the United States. Hundreds of U.S. military engineers were prepared to come to Venezuela's assistance but Chavez rejected their help because he believed their presence would perpetuate American domination in Latin America and the rest of the world. He did allow 120 U.S. soldiers to help with water purification projects.

During his 2000 visit to Iraq, Chavez met with Saddam Hussein (*front row, left*). (*AP Images/INA*)

Chavez further angered U.S. officials by refusing to allow their planes to track and pursue suspected drug smuggling flights in Venezuelan air space. He justified it by telling a reporter: "what would be the opinion of President Clinton if President Chavez asked for permission to conduct flights over Washington? We cannot violate our sovereignty."

In August 2000, Chavez angered both the U.S. and its allies during a tour of oil producing countries in the Middle East. He became the first head of state to visit Iraq since 1991, where he met with Saddam Hussein and said that the trade sanctions imposed on Iraq after the Persian Gulf War should be removed.

Chavez also traveled to Libya and met with Libyan dictator Muammar Qaddafi, considered by many nations in Europe and the U.S. to be a terrorist. He defended the meetings by saying that Iraq, Libya, and Venezuela are all OPEC members.

Perhaps the most disturbing aspect of Chavez's rule was his use of oil money to buy arms. He purchased AK-47 rifles and combat helicopters from Russia and made a tentative deal with Spain to buy $2 billion worth of military equipment. The U.S. worked to stop arm sales to Venezuela, but Chavez knew that if he had the money some nation would probably sell him the arms that he wanted.

Many Venezuelans began to worry that Chavez was assuming too much power too quickly. There was also resentment and concern over the time he was spending outside of Venezuela. Some of his opponents came to believe that a coup could quickly and effectively terminate Chavez's regime. By 2002, they were ready to give it a try.

five

Coup

In April 2002, a military coup removed Chavez from power. Pedro Carmona, a businessman and president of the Venezuelan Federation of Chambers of Commerce, replaced Chavez as president. Chavez has consistently maintained that the Bush Administration and the Central Intelligence Agency (CIA) orchestrated the revolt. There is evidence that the CIA had advance knowledge of the coup. A declassified U.S. intelligence brief dated April 6, 2002, described the political conditions in Caracas:

> Dissident military factions, including some disgruntled senior officers and a group of radical junior officers, are stepping up efforts to organize a coup against President Chavez, possibly as early as this month . . . [deleted] The level of detail in the reported plans . . .[deleted] targets Chavez and ten other senior officers for arrest.

The brief went on to lay out a scenario for how the coup could happen: "To provoke military action, the plotters may try to exploit unrest stemming from opposition demonstrations slated for later this month."

According to at least one source, coup leaders had made several visits to Washington, D.C., in the early months of 2002 and secured approval for overthrowing Chavez. Even if they did not participate in its planning or execution, it appears that U.S. officials made no effort to warn Chavez or any Venezuelan government official that a coup was in the works. Since the coup, the CIA has maintained that it was not their responsibility to warn Venezuelan government officials.

Prior to the coup, there had been a series of demonstrations and counter-demonstrations in Caracas. The anti-Chavez demonstrations had been brought on by Chavez's attempts to make sweeping changes in Venezuela's state-run oil company, *Petroleos de Venezuela* (PDVSA), which was resisting the president's efforts to bring it under stricter government control.

On April 8, 2002, Chavez fired seven of PDVSA's top executives and several other managers and officials, announcing the firings during a nationally televised speech. Anti-Chavez supporters called for a two-day strike to protest Chavez's proposed reforms. The strike was scheduled to occur on April 11 and 12.

On April 11, a large crowd of anti-Chavez protesters began marching from east Caracas to the PDVSA offices in the center of the city. The crowd, estimated at between 100,000 to 200,000, was redirected by labor leader Carlos Ortega to continue marching on to the presidential palace.

The re-routing of the march occurred without consulting police officials, who were supposed to approve the new

A large crowd of anti-Chavez protesters march to show their disapproval after Chavez fired workers from the state-run oil company, Petroleos de Venezuela. (*AP Images/Gregorio Marrero*)

route. There were also protests from the organizers of a pro-Chavez march that was going on at the time. The new route put the protesters on a collision course with the pro-Chavez demonstrators—and both sides were armed. The National Guard was loyal to Chavez; the Caracas Metropolitan Police were not. A confrontation ensued, shots were fired. Twenty people were killed, about one hundred more wounded. Most of the casualties were Chavez supporters, but who shot first and who was responsible for the deaths remain unanswered questions.

In later court testimony, police officers acknowledged that they had been ordered to fire at the crowd. That would have caused the National Guard and other Chavez supporters to return their fire.

Shortly after the deaths, some senior military officials turned against Chavez. Chavez had ordered troops to protect the presidential palace and secure the safety of the surrounding area. General Efrain Vasquez went on national television and called Chavez's order unconstitutional. Vasquez declared: "Mr. President, I was loyal to the end, but today's deaths cannot be tolerated."

After Vasquez's address, more officers joined in the plot to depose Chavez. A group of senior National Guard generals and navy admirals issued public statements calling Chavez's orders illegal.

Inside the palace, a worried Chavez tried to reverse the situation. He decided to make a nationally televised speech but the impact of the speech was blunted when four private stations used a split-screen image to belie Chavez's reassurances. They televised scenes of street violence outside the palace, while Chavez talked about having things under control.

After learning about the split-screen broadcasts, Chavez ordered the four private stations off the air. The stations refused to comply. Their broadcasts were blacked out in Caracas, but they continued broadcasting in the rest of Venezuela.

While some of his highest ranking officers were plotting against him, Chavez became a prisoner in the presidential palace. At around midnight on the April 11, Fidel Castro called Chavez with some timely advice. "Save your people and save yourself," Castro advised Chavez. "Do what you have to do. Negotiate with dignity. Do not sacrifice yourself."

Castro further advised that a surrender would be better than being killed in a coup.

After speaking to Castro, Chavez decided he would resign only if four conditions were met. His resignation would be presented to the National Assembly, the current constitution would still be honored and respected, the guaranteed physical safety all the people currently held captive in the presidential palace would be guaranteed, and safe passage out of the country would be provided for Chavez, his family, and his supporters.

Initially, the coup leaders agreed to Chavez's conditions, then rejected them. Whether Chavez ever formally resigned remains a matter of dispute. There's no written or recorded evidence to verify that he did, although the coup leaders announced that Chavez had resigned and took him into custody.

Outside of Venezuela, it was widely reported that Chavez had been removed from power. An editorial in the *New York Times* expressed relief that a dangerous tyrant had been supplanted: "With yesterday's resignation of President Hugo Chavez, Venezuelan democracy is no longer threatened by a would-be dictator. Mr. Chavez, a ruinous demagogue stepped down after the military intervened and handed power to a respected business leader, Pedro Carmona."

On April 12, Chavez was escorted under a military guard to Fort Tiuna, a military base controlled by the coup leaders. By then Chavez was aware that not all of the officers were solidly behind the coup. When the generals and other officers asked Chavez for his resignation, he firmly refused.

"I told them, with a serene voice that was a little louder than usual so that all could hear, they should think long and hard about what they were doing and what they planned to do—the responsibility that they were assuming with regard to Venezuela and the outside world—and I told them that I was not going to resign," Chavez said later. "They already had a piece of paper for me to sign, and I said that I was not going to so much as look at it."

Chavez then repeated his four conditions and said that because he was still the president he wasn't taking orders from them. He also told his captors that their coup would ultimately fail.

"I told them that I was not sure that they would be able to control the military," Chavez said, "and that I had talked to various commanders who had assured me that they would not accept a coup d' etat . . . I could see that I was catching their attention, since, clearly, some of them had been manipulated. Others began to take notice."

Once again, the officers rejected Chavez's conditions, and Chavez again reminded them he still was the president. He practically dared them to put him under arrest. While the impasse continued, Chavez got a couple of friendly soldiers guarding him to bring him a television and a telephone.

Chavez's oldest daughter, Maria Gabriella, is tearful while speaking to her father on the second day of his three-day removal from office. *(AP Images/APTN)*

The television news shows were reporting that Chavez had resigned and that the military was solidly behind the coup. Chavez phoned his wife, Marisabel, and his oldest daughter, Maria Gabriela, and told them to spread the news that he had not resigned. They contacted CNN and Castro with the news. Soon, CNN and Radio Havana were broadcasting that Chavez had not resigned. However, the news wasn't immediately broadcast in Caracas.

By midday Friday, Chavez was watching a television broadcast of Pedro Carmona being sworn in as Venezuela's new president. Carmona announced that his new regime was going to close down the National Assembly and the Supreme Court, abolish the constitution, and remove mayors and state governors from office.

In this photo, Pedro Carmona is being sworn in as president. (*AP Images/ Fernando Llano*)

Chavez realized that Carmona had made a mistake by trying to do too much, too quickly. Carmona's power grab cost him the support of most of the military and many Venezuelans outside of the military were concerned that Carmona was setting himself up to be a dictator.

On Friday night, Chavez was moved to a naval base northwest of Caracas. He didn't know if he was going to be deported or executed. When he woke up on Saturday, April 13, soldiers at the naval base began asking him why he resigned. Chavez told them that he hadn't. After Chavez told a young lieutenant that he had never resigned, the officer said: "Then, you are still the president and these people have violated the constitution. They are deceiving us."

The lieutenant told Chavez that the commander of a parachute regiment had refused to obey orders issued by the new government. Chavez asked the lieutenant if other military units were defying Carmona.

"I don't know," the lieutenant answered, "but those of us here are with you." He told Chavez that he and other soldiers at the naval base were planning to free him from his captors. But before they could put their plan in action, Chavez was moved again. This time his captors moved him to La Orchila, a small island north of Venezuela.

While Chavez was being moved around, thousands of demonstrators were milling outside of the presidential palace, demanding that Chavez be returned to power. Inside the palace, Carmona and his supporters nervously watched the growing crowd that had already surrounded the palace and the streets leading to it.

Then, the leader of Chavez's Honor Guard ordered his men to seize the palace. By that time, Carmona had left, but many of his supporters were captured and detained by the Honor Guard. Carmona had gone to Fort Tiuna to meet with some of the military officers that had supported the coup. He discovered that their support was wavering; some officers complained that they had been deceived by the coup leaders and asked for evidence verifying that Chavez had resigned.

Fort Tiuna was also surrounded by demonstrators demanding that Chavez be reinstated as president. General Garcia Carneiro decided to address the pro-Chavez demonstrators.

He climbed on top of a tank grasping a microphone and quieted the demonstrators by making a surprising announcement. Carnerio declared that the armed forces were no longer recognizing Carmona as president. He said that the military would do everything they could to guarantee that Chavez would be returned to power.

Around seven o'clock on Saturday night, Carmona and some of the key officers who had supported the coup were arrested. After being arrested, Carmona asked what crime he had committed and was told that he had "violated the Constitution of the Republic."

Emboldened supporters of Chavez took over television stations that hadn't reported any news about the demonstrations and uprisings. Around 2 a.m. on Sunday the media began reporting that Chavez would be returning to the presidential palace. Chavez arrived there around 3:45 a.m. About fifteen minutes later, he was giving a speech on national TV. Chavez joked that he knew that he would be returning to power, but he never imagined that it would happen so quickly.

At the onset, the coup looked like it was well-planned and smoothly executed, yet it collapsed in about forty-eight hours. The main reason cited for the quick collapse is that the planners made two major miscalculations. The first mistake was that the coup leaders thought they could ignore Carlos Ortega and organized labor. When the coup leaders formed a cabinet for the new government, they excluded organized labor and practically all the moderate opposition parties that had opposed Chavez. This attempt at a too rapid return to the old system undermined military support for the new government.

The second major mistake was that the coup leader's underestimated Chavez's popular support among both ordinary

A triumphant Chavez waves to supporters on the night of his return to office. *(AP Images/APTN)*

citizens and the military. When a crowd of around 100,000 demonstrators surrounded the presidential palace, the coup leaders were taken aback.

After resuming power, Chavez was forgiving of the people who had conspired to overthrow him. He announced that there would be no reprisals against them. Following the announcement, Ortega and several of the coconspirators returned to Venezuela.

Chavez did remove around four hundred mostly senior officers and replaced them with loyal supporters. In August 2002, Venezuela's Supreme Court ruled that four high-ranking officers who were charged with rebellion could not be tried. By an 11-9 margin, the high court decreed that a coup did not occur and ruled that the officers intervened to fill a "power vacuum" brought on by the announcement of Chavez's resignation.

Since resuming power, Chavez has consistently maintained that the Bush administration was secretly behind the failed coup. If it was, the nature and extent of its involvement has remained a secret. However, there was no question that the Bush administration would like to see Chavez removed.

Only hours after the coup, American officials were blaming the uprising on Chavez. White House spokesman Ari Fleischer said that "the Chavez government provoked the crisis." That view was shared by Philip Reeker, a U.S. State Department spokesman who said that "undemocratic actions committed or encouraged by the Chavez government provoked the crisis." The U.S. did not condemn the coup until it became apparent that Chavez would return to power.

After the anti-Chavez movement found that it couldn't remove him by a military coup, they conspired to create economic chaos by shutting down the state owned and operated Petroleos de Venezuela.

The state-owned PDVSA had been run for the benefit of its managers and employees. Its profits had been invested outside of Venezuela and it was preparing to be privatized before Chavez's 1999 constitution blocked the action.

In December 2002, an estimated 19,000 PDSVA employees went on strike. Most were skilled workers in jobs related to refining, finances, exploration, production, and transportation. It looked like the PDVSA would have a serious personnel shortage, but skilled replacements weren't hard to find. "Despite the loss of all these employees, among who were highly specialized people with long experience in the corporation, workers of the company were able to substitute for them," said Ali Rodriquez, Chavez's energy minister. "A characteristic of the oil industry has been that in many cases people retire in their prime and go to work for other companies."

Even with skilled replacements, oil exports dropped from 2.5 million barrels a day to less than 2 million in the month of December 2002. Brazilian president Fernando Henrique Cardoso came to Chavez's aid by sending an emergency shipment of 520,000 barrels of gasoline to Venezuela.

Workers loyal to Chavez worked overtime. Other workers boycotted the strike because of a sense of patriotism and devotion to duty. "Basically we are all Venezuelans," said oil worker Cipiriano Hernandez. "We love our country and we do not want to see it fall."

Despite long lines at gas stations, food shortages, and protest marches, Chavez defeated the strikers. His only apparent concession was an agreement to face a recall referendum in 2004.

In mid-August 2004, his opponents gathered enough signatures on a petition to force a nationwide referendum to decide if he should be removed from office. By a decisive 58 to 42 percent margin, Venezuelans voted to keep Chavez in office.

Opposition spokesman Henry Ramos angrily said: "They have perpetrated a gigantic fraud against the will of the people." Ramos's charges were rebutted by former U.S. president Jimmy Carter, whose organization, the Carter Center, monitored the results along with representatives from the Organization of American States. Both organizations had been invited by the Chavez government and the opposition to verify the results. "There is a clear difference in favor of the government of President Chavez," Carter said. The former president added that all Venezuelans should accept the results: "unless there is tangible proof that the reports are incorrect."

Chavez's win was seen as a setback for the Bush administration. The U.S. State Department waited for more than a day before acknowledging that it backed the "preliminary results." Two days later State Department spokesman Adam Ereli dodged questions from reporters on why the U.S. had not conveyed its congratulations to Chavez.

Former president Carter didn't express any support for Chavez, but he hoped that the election results would somehow temper Chavez's attitudes towards the United States. "I would hope that President Chavez would now cool that anti-U.S. rhetoric," Carter said. "There is no doubt that Chavez is a charismatic figure, very fiery in his rhetoric, which I deplore. But that's his personal characteristic, one of the avenues of his popularity among Venezuelans. I think now, though, that he is not campaigning for anything."

Chavez exulted in his latest victory. While his opposition fragmented and shrank, he was free to engage in forging alliances and making oil deals with other nations.

six

International Allies and Enemies

T hroughout his presidency, Chavez has sought to expand his influence outside of Venezuela and find allies for supporting and expanding his "Bolivarian Revolution." He has tried to influence elections in Mexico, and in Central and Latin America. The heads of state in Cuba, Bolivia, Nicaragua, and Ecuador are all his allies, but in other countries and elections, Chavez has been rebuffed.

When Alan Garcia eked out a narrow victory in Peru's presidential election in June 2006, he acknowledged Chavez's attempts to influence the election: "Tonight, the country has sent a message of sovereignty and national independence and defeated Senor Hugo Chavez's efforts to incorporate us in his expansionist strategy."

Chavez had strongly supported Ollanta Humala, a former army officer and had denounced Garcia by saying: "I pray to God that he won't become president." Chavez had even threatened to break off diplomatic relations with Peru if

Garcia were elected, but later backed off from that threat.

There were accusations, but no proof, that Chavez had been bankrolling the campaigns of left-wing parties in Peru as well as assorted street protests by different social movements. There is still concern that Chavez will use his influence to undermine Garcia's presidency, and that Humala has enough power and influence to make the southern Andes region of Peru ungovernable.

Garcia has taken action to minimize Chavez's influence in Latin America. Between his election and his inauguration, he visited the presidents of Brazil, Chile, Colombia, and Ecuador in an attempt to forge an alliance against Chavez.

Alan Garcia, president of Peru, has attempted to lessen Chavez's influence over Latin American politics. *(AP Images/Martin Mejia)*

Venezuela and the U.S. became locked in a battle to see which nation will exert the greatest influence over Uruguay's leftist government. The Bush Administration offered Uruguay a free trade agreement that would allow them to increase exports of meat, leather, and cheese to the U.S. Venezuela has countered by giving Uruguay discounted petroleum products and pledging to invest an estimated $500 million to build an oil refinery in Uruguay.

Chavez has also aided Uruguay by giving them enough money to keep some unprofitable businesses afloat. Direct aid to glass, tire, and sugar plants has saved hundreds of jobs. Most recently, Chavez has offered financial support to prop up a government financial cooperative that makes small loans to Uruguayan businesses and citizens.

In March 2005, Chavez announced that Venezuela would provide Uruguay with 40,000 barrels of oil per day. The two countries agreed to a twenty-five-year deal. Two-thirds of the oil would be paid for with milk and meat, the other one-third would be paid off by low interest loans. "It [the oil for food deal] doesn't cost Chavez a lot of money, but it generates a lot of good will," noted Danilo Abrilla, a Uruguayan writer. "That way when he comes here, he's solved people's problems, and they will go out for him."

Along with the free trade agreement, the United States has offered to build a medical and dental clinic in Montevideo, Uruguay's capital. Uruguayan groups aligned with Chavez have claimed that the offer is just an American plot to establish a military presence in their country.

At present, Uruguay is enjoying the attention from both countries. Their president, Tabare Vazquez would like to expand trade with the U.S., but he's opposed by some

Chavez with Tabare Vazquez, president of Uruguay *(AP Images/Alejandro Arigon)*

anti-U.S. coalitions within his government that are aligned with supporters of Chavez.

In Ecuador, Chavez supported presidential candidate Rafael Correa. After his victory, Correa exceeded even Chavez in the vehemence of his denouncements of U.S. President Bush. After Chavez attacked Bush at the United Nations as "the devil," Correa said that the devil himself should be offended by the comparison, and added that Bush was "tremendously dimwitted."

Nixon in Venezuela

When Hugo Chavez called U.S. president George W. Bush "the devil" in a 2006 speech at the United Nations, it wasn't the first time that relations between the United States and Venezuela have been strained.

In May 1958, U.S. vice-president Richard M. Nixon was touring Latin America. Nixon, who would later serve as president from 1969 to 1974, was greeted by angry protestors when his plane landed at Maiquetia airport outside of Caracas, Venezuela.

About four months prior to Nixon's visit, Venezuelans had deposed President Marcos Perez Jimenez, a ruthless and corrupt dictator. The U.S. granted Jimenez political asylum and Jimenez settled in Miami. Furthermore, during his reign, the U.S. had honored Jimenez by awarding him their Legion of Merit military medal. The Venezuelan people were enraged at the U.S.'s honoring of Jimenez, and they focused their anger on Nixon, the visiting American representative.

The crowd waiting to confront Nixon was the largest of his Latin American tour. When they spotted him, they began chanting, "GO HOME NIXON: YANKEE IMPERIALIST." Other protestors shouted obscenities at the vice-president and members of his party.

While they were walking out of the airport, Nixon and his wife, Pat, were repeatedly spat upon by the protestors. According to Nixon's Spanish speaking translator, Vernon Walters, the Venezuelan police did nothing to shield or protect the Nixons.

En route to Caracas, the Nixon motorcade encountered roadblocks. That allowed more protestors to kick the fenders and doors of Nixon's car. Venezuelan police and U.S. Secret Service agents dispersed the protestors. A later roadblock once again halted the motorcade; this time, protestors armed with sticks, rocks, and pieces of pipe began beating Nixon's limousine. They smashed three windows before the Secret Service agents drew their revolvers.

A tear gas bomb dispersed the mob. Nixon canceled a scheduled appearance to lay a wreath at the tomb of Simon Bolivar. The vice-president and his entourage opted to seek safety at the U.S. embassy in Caracas. Because of a communications mistake, U.S. President Dwight D. Eisenhower became concerned that the American embassy might be under attack.

U.S. Navy vessels were summoned to the area. When Nixon left Caracas, there was a U.S. Navy carrier, cruiser, and six destroyers stationed thirty miles off of the coast of Venezuela.

In 1963, Jimenez was finally extradited back to Venezuela. The former president was convicted and imprisoned on embezzlement charges. Jimenez was released in 1968 and exiled to Spain. He died there in 2001.

Alvaro Noboa has been Correa's major rival for the presidency. A Swiss-educated billionaire, Noboa has been unsuccessful in two prior bids for the presidency. His platform has called for limiting political ties with Venezuela and negotiating a free trade agreement with the U.S.

Correa's popularity rose after he began criticizing U.S. influence in Ecuador. He had strongly opposed a free trade agreement with the United States and said he would no longer allow the U.S. military to use an air base in Manta on Ecuador's Pacific coast that had been used for drug surveillance flights. "We can negotiate with the U.S. about a base in Manta," Correa said, "and if they let us put a military base in Miami, if there is no problem, we'll accept."

Correa made a surprisingly weak showing during the first round of voting in mid-October 2006. He received around 22 percent of the votes to Noboa's 27 percent. Correa said that fraud may have caused an inaccurate tabulation, but most observers blamed his close ties with Chavez for his weak showing. There were thirteen candidates running and eleven were eliminated after the first election. Noboa exploited Correa's close ties with Chavez by calling him a "friend of terrorists, a friend of Chavez, a friend of Cuba."

After the first round of voting, Correa changed his campaign tactics. He began emphasizing domestic issues, such as affordable housing and helping the poor by giving them cash subsidies. The changes led to a victory in the election's second round, when he received around 57 percent of the vote to Noboa's 43 percent.

Chavez stands beside Rafael Correa, president of Ecuador. *(AP Images/ Santiago Armas)*

Correa's election had U.S. officials worried. During the election, Correa called for renegotiating the country's foreign debt and ending the air base agreement. But since his election, Correa has softened the tone of his anti-U.S. and anti-Bush rhetoric. "We love the American people and its government, aside from the criticism we might have of that government," Correa said. "It's nothing personal against Bush," Correa added. "I just don't agree with his thinking."

Correa hopes to emulate Chavez and establish a new constitution that would increase his power at the expense of Ecuador's Congress. Passing a new constitution will be difficult because Correa has few supporters in Congress. Ecuador's Congress also has a history of ousting presidents and it is not likely they'll want to give up that power.

In an extremely close and bitterly contested Mexican presidential election, attack ads featuring Chavez helped determine the outcome. Winning candidate Felipe Calderon negatively linked his opponent, Andres Manuel Lopez Obrador, with the Venezuelan president. Some of the ads showed unflattering pictures of Lopez Obrador paired with photos of Chavez. The most negative ad showed Chavez surrounded by soldiers and machine guns and was accompanied by a voice-over saying: "In Mexico, you don't have to die to define your future—you only have to vote!"

An article in the *Washington Post* analyzed the ads: "The strategy of Lopez Obrador's opponents has been clear. By linking the candidate to Chavez, they have tried to frighten voters into believing Lopez Obrador will be a carbon copy of the Venezuelan president who has been accused of crushing dissent and crippling democratic institutions."

Chavez and Evo Morales display copies of a trade agreement between Venezuela and Bolivia. *(AP Images/Dado Galdieri)*

It's a truism of politics that voters don't like negative attack ads. It's also true that candidates continue to use them because they work. In this case, the negative ads linking Lopez Obrador with Chavez helped Calderon eke out a narrow win.

In the South American nation of Bolivia, Chavez has a staunch ally in president Evo Morales, who was elected in December 2005. Morales had run and lost in 2002 and during that election Chavez was accused of offering Morales a campaign donation of $300,000, a charge Chavez denied. Between the 2002 loss and 2005 victory, Chavez stayed in close contact with Morales.

Morales's background and political views have made him a cause for concern for the United States. Morales is a former cocoa leaf farmer; cocoa is a key ingredient in the manufacture of cocaine. In Bolivia and other Latin American countries, the native people have historically used coca leaves for religious ceremonies and for medicinal purposes. Morales has said that he supports the production of the leaves for religious ceremonies and for use in herbal teas that are openly sold in Bolivia, but opposes the production of cocaine. This position won him wide support among Bolivians, while also earning him the contempt of U.S. law officers fighting cocaine production and trafficking.

In 2005, Morales ended his presidential campaign in the region of Chapare, which produces around 90 percent of Bolivia's cocoa crop. Chapare had been targeted by the U.S. Drug Enforcement Agency (DEA), and there had been heated clashes between the natives and agents from the DEA working with Bolivian authorities. During his campaign stop, Morales denounced the clashes: "In the Chapare there have been confrontations . . . between U.S. soldiers and Quechua and Aymara indigenous people who resist. From our point of view this is unconstitutional and illegal."

U.S. authorities have tried to reduce coca production by providing Bolivians with alternate crops, such as coffee and bananas. This hasn't worked because coca production is much more lucrative—the alternate crops earn as little as one-tenth of what coca sells for.

The U.S. has threatened to greatly reduce foreign aid to Bolivia if coca production isn't sharply reduced. Bolivians have resented those threats and they blame the American demand for cocaine for the large coca crop. "If they want to talk about the war on drugs, fine," Morales said. "But the discussion should start with demand and not supply. If they cut demand we'll work to cut supply. But at the moment it's not the traffickers that are in jail, it's the farmers."

Most recently, political opponents of Morales have been critical of the growing military relationship between Venezuela and Bolivia. In late December 2006, around thirty Venezuelan military officers entered Bolivia without the approval of Bolivia's Congress. Walker San Miguel, Bolivia's defense minister, said the Venezuelan officers were in Bolivia to assist in the piloting and maintenance of two helicopters that Chavez had given to Morales for his use while traveling within Bolivia. Venezuela's defense minister defended the presence of the soldiers by saying it could be considered to be "humanitarian aid."

As U.S. influence in Bolivia has waned, Chavez has provided Bolivia with around $50 million in loans for military spending. Venezuela has also assisted Bolivia in building border posts in its eastern lowlands, an area that has been seeking more political autonomy from Morales's rule. Critics of Morales have claimed that the outposts and increased military presence are an attempt to intimidate them.

A further outcry against Morales's government was caused by remarks made by Julio Montes, Venezuela's ambassador to Bolivia, who said that if a crisis arose, Venezuela would consider using military intervention to aid Morales. Montes later amended his remarks by saying he was referring to general assistance and not the deployment of Venezuelan troops.

Chavez's admiration for Cuba's Fidel Castro, and a shared love of baseball, solidified an alliance between Chavez and Castro, who has been in power since he led a Communist revolution in Cuba in the late 1950s. However, Castro, who

Chavez sits with his friend and mentor, Fidel Castro, in this 2001 photograph. *(AP Images/Jose Goitia)*

is now in his ninth decade of life, has begun to suffer failing health and a change of leadership in Cuba could alter its close ties with Venezuela.

In November 1999, Chavez traveled to Cuba to improve Venezuelan-Cuban relations. Chavez and Castro both "coached" baseball teams in a series of friendly exhibition games in Havana that were widely broadcast throughout Latin America.

Prior to the games, Chavez spoke at the University of Havana. With Castro listening, Chavez said: "Venezuela is traveling towards the same sea as the Cuban people, a sea of happiness and of real social justice and peace." Then he paused and turned to Castro and called the Cuban leader a "brother" and said that he was seeking unity between the two nations. "Here we are, as alert as ever, Fidel and Hugo, fighting with dignity and courage to defend the interests of our people, and to bring alive the ideas of Bolivar and Marti. (Jose Marti, 1853-1895, was a Cuban writer and revolutionary who fought to free Cuba from Spanish rule.) In the name of Cuba and of Venezuela, I appeal for the unity of our two peoples, and of the revolutions that we both lead."

Chavez's effusive praise for Castro wasn't surprising. While he was imprisoned, Chavez was an avid reader, and Castro and his revolution and rule of Cuba was a subject he studied. "I read a lot of books about Fidel," Chavez said, and has been inspired by Castro's life. He claims that during his imprisonment, he decided "My God, when I get out of here I am going to have to get to know Fidel."

In exchange for Venezuelan oil, Castro has sent doctors to Venezuela to provide health care and medical services in the country's poorest areas. The oil for doctors' exchange has also enabled thousands of Venezuelans to travel to Cuba for eye surgery.

Cuba and Venezuela have also established strong military ties. In November 1999, Chavez and Venezuelan military leaders visited Cuba to have what was called an "exchange of experiences" with Cuban officials. The Caracas newspaper, *El Universal*, reported in late 2001 that the military relationship between the two countries was very tight. Since then, Venezuelan troops have gone to Cuba to participate in joint military maneuvers with their hosts.

Once Castro is gone, Cuba will still be dependent on Venezuela for oil. As Cuba's new government probably won't risk alienating Chavez, the two countries are likely to remain allies. Jorge R. Pinon, a senior research associate at the University of Miami, has analyzed why Cuba and Venezuela will maintain friendly relations: "Chavez could say, 'If you change your ways, I'll stop delivering oil.' That's a trump card because without Venezuelan oil the system would collapse."

Chavez has also worked to establish closer ties with nations outside of Latin America. While visiting Beijing, China, in September 2006, he signed an agreement to triple Venezuela's oil exports to China. China in turn, agreed to invest more money in Chinese state-owned oil companies doing business in Venezuela. China's booming economy has dramatically increased its oil imports. Chavez has talked about China replacing the United States as the top importer of Venezuelan oil.

Following Chavez's reelection in December 2006, the *New York Times* reported that leftist candidates had won presidential elections in Brazil, Ecuador, Nicaragua, and Venezuela. Among the leftist presidents in Latin America, the *Times* called Chavez: ". . . not necessarily its most representative figure. But he is its most vocal one, especially when it comes to chiding President Bush."

As the U.S. and its allies grow increasingly concerned about the stability of the Middle East as a reliable source of oil, there's a general agreement that Chavez's international influence and importance has grown and will continue to grow.

Thus far, the biggest setback that Chavez has suffered occurred at the United Nations. Venezuela had been vying for the rotating seat on the UN's Security Council and Chavez had lobbied hard for the seat. The Security Council is made up of five permanent members—the U.S., China, Russia, France and Great Britain—and ten temporary seats that are held for two years by nations selected from designated regions by the General Assembly. If Venezuela won a two-year seat on the Security Council, Chavez would have a powerful forum to be used to attack the U.S. and to extol the virtues of his leadership in his own country as well as his influence throughout the world.

Chavez traveled the globe promising aid and discounted oil in exchange for promises of support in the UN. Before the voting on Venezuela's bid for a Security Council seat began, Chavez predicted he would win the seat over U.S.-backed Guatemala. He was confident the votes of the members of the Caribbean Community, the Arab League, the African Union, and five other Latin American countries were committed to Venezuela. Russia and China were also said to be backing Venezuela.

The United Nations has 192 member nations and a two-thirds vote (128) is required for election to the Security Council. After the first round of voting, Guatemala led Venezuela, 109 to seventy-six. After forty-seven indecisive ballots, both countries were forced to drop out of the race. Both agreed to back Panama as a compromise choice.

Venezuela's ambassador to the UN blamed the defeat on American "bribes" and pressure. However, it is clear that Chavez overestimated his support. Also, many political analysts said that Chavez's denunciation of President Bush as "the Devil" in a September 2006 speech at the UN backfired. Experts on the UN claim that the disrespect for UN protocol that Chavez exhibited offended other leaders who worried that Chavez might be misrepresenting third world views.

Mexico's ambassador, Enrique Berruga, agreed that Chavez's speech went too far and doomed Venezuela's chances of winning the election. "The speech really hurt his case," Berruga said. "Most members don't want this place to be turned into a mockery. In the General Assembly, there are limits and he went way beyond them."

Chavez's friendship with Iran was cited as one reason the moderate Arab states voted against Venezuela, and several votes from Asian nations were reportedly lost because Chavez refused to denounce North Korea's pursuit of nuclear weapons.

Even after the rebuff in the UN, Chavez gave no indication he would tone down his inflammatory anti-U.S. rhetoric. He also stepped up his attempt to forge alliances with enemies of the U.S.

In late August 2006, Chavez traveled to Damascus, Syria, and met Syrian president Bashar Assad at his presidential palace. During Chavez's visit, delegates from Venezuela and Syria signed a total of thirteen economic and political agreements. Assad also pledged to support Venezuela's candidacy for a seat on the UN Security Council. In return, Chavez offered to help Assad build an oil refinery in Syria.

After their meeting, both leaders denounced "American imperialism" and agreed to work together to end it. "No matter how strong the American empire becomes and no matter how much force it uses, it will be defeated," Chavez predicted. "We and Syria as well as other countries will be an army of tigers, struggling and strong."

Chavez went even further by saying that he would single handedly end "American imperialism": "It must be said to the peoples of the world, and it must be said to imperialism itself that in this twenty-first century I will dig the grave of U.S. imperialism."

Before leaving Damascus, Chavez also called for Israel to withdraw its troops from Lebanon and to end its blockade of that country. Earlier in the month, Chavez had recalled Venezuela's ambassador to Israel; Israel responded by removing their ambassador to Venezuela and criticized Chavez for making "wild slurs" and his "one-sided policy" in the Middle East.

Before visiting Syria, Chavez received a pledge of mutual support from Iranian president, Mahmoud Ahmadinejad, who has gone so far as to claim that the Holocaust—the attempt by the German Nazi regime to murder all the Jews in Europe during World War II—was a myth. After Chavez stated that "We will back Iran any time, in any situation," Iran's state-run television quoted Ahmadinejad as saying, "I feel I have met a brother and trench mate after meeting Chavez. We think Iran and Venezuela should share all experiences of each other, stay by each other and they have to be supporters of each other."

As long as he is in power in Venezuela, it seems assured that Chavez will continue to use his country's oil reserves to make deals with other countries who are enemies of the U.S.

seven

Destroying the Opposition

S ince he survived the coup in 2002, and the recall referendum in 2004, opposition to Chavez in Venezuela has been fragmented and largely leaderless. In addition, high oil prices have fueled the economy and bankrolled Chavez's social programs, winning him the support of the nation's poorest citizens.

After losing the referendum, Chavez's opponents accused him of election fraud but were unable to offer any proof to support their accusations. Opposition to Chavez became even weaker when many opposition parties pulled out of the December 2005 National Assembly elections after claiming that the National Electoral Council (NEC) was biased against them.

After the opposition parties boycotted the elections, the newly elected National Assembly didn't have a single member who was publicly opposed to Chavez. The new National Assembly then took steps to help ensure Chavez's reelection in December 2006. The legislative body chose a new five-member board for the election commission. The new board was composed of four Chavez supporters and one token member of the opposition. They supported the continued use of fingerprinting machines for checking voter's identities. Opponents of Chavez have claimed fingerprinting voters compromises the secrecy of the ballots.

The new election commission also refused to count paper ballots. The only acceptable ballots would be the ones cast on voting machines. There was also controversy over the large expansion of registered voters. From 2004 to 2006, the number of registered voters increased by 2 million. When a group of independent universities offered to audit the voter lists the commission rejected their offer.

By late July of 2006, there were about a dozen opposition candidates to challenge Chavez, but none of them looked like a serious contender. In one poll of voter preferences, "someone new" (17 percent) and "none of the above" (10 percent) finished second and third in the opinion poll. Even Henry Ramos, the leader of Venezuela's once powerful Democratic Action party, called the group of opposition candidates "drunks fighting over an empty bottle."

On August 9, 2006, nine of the declared presidential candidates opposing Chavez dropped out of the race, which led to the primary election being canceled. The nine former candidates united to endorse Manuel Rosales, the governor of the Venezuelan state of Zuila, for president. While accepting their support, Rosales accused Chavez of spending too much money on a military buildup and pledged that a greater share of Venezuela's oil wealth would go to health care, education, and helping the poor. He addressed complaints that Chavez has increased the divide between his poor supporters and wealthy

Manuel Rosales ran against Chavez in the 2006 presidential election but only received 37 percent of the popular vote. *(AP Images/Leslie Mazoch)*

opponents by saying: "I will be president of all Venezuelans regardless of their differences."

Three days later, Chavez confidently declared his candidacy for reelection. In his remarks he accused the United States of trying to destabilize Venezuela by undermining the upcoming election and presented himself as the popular choice and as the candidate of change, instead of the status quo. "I am the candidate of the revolution," Chavez declared, "and without a doubt I am the candidate of the national majority, of those who continue transforming the country and saving it from the capitalist quagmire."

Shortly after Chavez's reelection announcement, an unlikely third candidate entered the race. Benjamin Rausseo had gained fame as Venezuela's best-known stand up comedian, but he insisted that his candidacy was no joke. While being vague on his campaign objectives, Rausseo said that he would be less militaristic and confrontational than Chavez. "We differ," Rausseo said, "in that I'd exchange guns for books and represent a rupture from this idea that Venezuela, a peaceful country, has to go around confronting the world."

Still, Rausseo's candidacy was short-lived. Around mid-November he withdrew from the race. In his withdrawal announcement, Rausseo tacitly acknowledged that it wasn't the right time for him to be seeking the presidency. "I have a vision for the country," Rausseo said, "but right now the conditions are not apt for me to be president."

With Rausseo out of the race, Chavez maintained a comfortable double-digit lead over Rosales. Regardless of his lead, he used all the power of his office to help ensure his reelection. As president, Chavez was allowed unlimited air time on Venezuela's broadcast media; during the campaign Chavez had twenty-two times as much television time as Rosales.

Chavez also reportedly threatened the 40,000 workers in Venezuela's state-run oil industry with losing their jobs if they failed to vote for him. Members of the military received similar threats. An estimated 1 million government workers received bonuses prior to the election. It was made clear that anyone who received a government paycheck was expected to vote for Chavez.

Chavez campaigned without using Rosales's name. Instead, he ran against the Bush Administration. He said the true choice was between him and George W. Bush, not between him and his opponent. President Bush refrained from making any public comments about the Venezuelan election. However, it has been reported that since 2002, the United States has channeled millions of dollars to Venezuelan organizations that have been critical of Chavez. U.S. officials responded by saying that the money was used to bring supporters and opponents of Chavez together for political discussions.

The underdog Rosales campaigned hard, attacking Chavez for his militarism, Venezuela's high poverty level, and rising crime rate. He advocated a plan for getting more of Venezuela's oil revenues to 3 million of the country's poorest citizens and accused Chavez of failing to deliver the oil wealth to the poor.

Chavez responded by citing figures showing that the poverty level has decreased during his presidency. Venezuelan

A Venezuelan woman carries discounted food that is delivered by a government truck emblazoned with Chavez's image and the words, "A plan to fight against inflated prices, a decision of President Hugo Chavez." Chavez claims that the poverty level has decreased during his presidency. *(AP Images/Leslie Mazoch)*

government statistics say that in 1998, the year before Chavez took office, the poverty rate was 44 percent and that by 2006 it had declined to 34 percent.

Chavez supporters and some economists dismissed Rosales' plan of wealth redistribution as expensive and potentially ruinous for Venezuela's economy. There were reminders of how falling oil prices in the 1980s abruptly ended the large scale social programs and infrastructure projects of President Carlos Perez. "We're living in a period of political amnesia with an inability to remember the crisis in the 80s when oil prices crashed," said economist Michael Penfold-Becerra.

According to an estimate by Barclay's Capital, every $1 drop in the price per barrel of oil causes a $1 billion drop in Venezuela's national income. In July 2006, oil prices peaked at $78.40 a barrel. By November 2006, oil prices were down 25 percent. Yet, even with that large decrease, Venezuela's economy was doing quite well. In the week before the election, the Caracas stock exchange reported a 129.2 percent rise for 2006. On the Friday before Election Day, the exchange's main index had an 8 percent increase, the biggest daily gain in four years. Also in 2006, there was an 84 percent increase in bank deposits in Venezuela. "For all of Chavez's faults, his government has been extremely pragmatic in economic terms," noted Venezuelan economist, Jose Guerra. "State-supported capitalism isn't just surviving under Chavez. It is thriving."

Even Chavez's opponents and detractors couldn't claim that the economy was weak. Economic indicators and predictions said that Venezuela's economic growth in 2006 would exceed 10 percent. The *New York Times* reported that

Venezuela's economy was "the fastest-growing economy in the Americas."

Unfortunately, while the economy was booming so was Venezuela's crime rate. Since Chavez took office in 1999, homicides have increased 67 percent. Venezuela also reports one of the highest rates of gun-related deaths in Latin America, 41.4 per every 100,000 people. Rosales hammered away at the crime issue, while Chavez largely ignored it.

In the end, the soaring crime rate didn't help Rosales or hurt Chavez. Political analysts said that Chavez's use of government handouts, such as subsidized groceries and health care, allowed Venezuelans to ignore the rise in crime. "Chavez has shielded himself from the issue because people see his government as an important arbiter in their daily life," said Miguel Tinker-Salas, a college professor and expert on Venezuelan history. "Chavez's policies have made a difference among the poor, and that's what is recognized."

Three days before the election, things took a strange turn when Chavez claimed that Venezuelan authorities had thwarted an assassination attempt against Rosales. During a lengthy press conference, Chavez said that "fascist militants" were going to assassinate Rosales while he was giving a speech. Chavez further claimed that the militants would blame the assassination on his administration in hopes of derailing the election. Most observers were convinced there was no assassination conspiracy and that Chavez staged the entire episode to win votes.

On election eve, Chavez was still enjoying a substantial lead over Rosales. Some pollsters said that it was twenty percentage points. One magazine article analyzed why Chavez remained such a heavy favorite:

> Mr. Chavez has some powerful advantages. He is an instinctive political communicator with an almost magical rapport with his supporters. He is reaping the benefits of a huge oil windfall: although output has fallen, higher prices have quadrupled the value of Venezuela's oil exports since 1998. . . . Mr. Chavez has channeled some of the oil money to social programmes (called "missions") which provide health care, education and subsidized food in poor areas that were previously neglected by the creaking welfare state.

On Election Day approximately 70 percent of Venezuela's registered voters cast ballots. The final returns gave Chavez 63 percent of the votes to 37 percent for Rosales. Rosales had done a bit better than most forecasts had predicted, but it was a decisive win for Chavez. The 63 percent he received was an improvement over the 56 percent he got in 1998. In the 2004 recall referendum, there had been about 4 million anti-Chavez votes cast. That was roughly the same number that Rosales received in 2006. Chavez carried all twenty-four Venezuelan states, including Rosales' home state of Zulia.

Rosales quickly conceded his loss, but he pledged to lead the opposition to Chavez. "We recognize that today they defeated us," Rosales told his loyal supporters. "We will continue in this struggle."

After Rosales' concession, Chavez stood on the balcony of the presidential palace and touted his reelection as a victory for socialism and as a repudiation of the Bush administration. "Long live the revolution," he shouted to his cheering supporters. "Venezuela demonstrated that a new and better world is possible, and we are building it."

Then, Chavez began denouncing President George W. Bush. "It's another defeat for the devil who tries to dominate

In recent years, Chavez has become more overtly religious. He is being blessed by Pope Benedict XVI in this 2006 photo. *(AP Images/Miraflores Press Office/Juan Carlos Solorzano)*

the world," Chavez told his adoring followers. "Down with imperialism! We need a new world!"

The most puzzling remarks Chavez made that evening were the ones with strong religious overtones. Although he was raised as a Catholic, Chavez is not a regular churchgoer. However, recently he has begun mentioning Jesus Christ almost as much as Simon Bolivar. "The Kingdom of Christ is the kingdom of love, of peace; the kingdom of justice, of solidarity, brotherhood, the kingdom of socialism," he told the cheering crowd below the balcony. "This is the kingdom of the future of Venezuela."

Some political analysts speculate that Chavez may be starting to think of himself as a messiah, a charge Chavez has denied. Chavez told an interviewer that he wasn't "Christian or Catholic." Instead, analysts believe that Chavez merely uses religion as a way to serve his needs. "He's religious in the way that it serves his political project."

An impoverished man accepts a handout from a passerby in front of graffiti that reads, "Chavez until year 2021." Chavez has stated that he would like to remain president until 2021. (*AP Images/Leslie Mazoch*)

Barring unforeseen circumstances, Chavez will continue to serve as president until 2012. At present, no one expects him to leave office willingly. He has said that he wants to change the constitution to eliminate presidential term limits. Because his opposition has no seats in Venezuela's National Assembly, it is very likely he will be able to alter the constitution to give him the possibility of ruling for life. He might also hold a nationwide constitutional referendum to get approval of a new constitution that would remove term limits on the presidency.

An article in the *Economist* magazine explained why Chavez may easily become president for life. "The president's power looks limitless. Because the opposition chose to boycott a legislative election last year, it has no representatives in the National Assembly. The government controls the judiciary and all the other institutions of state."

eight

Uncertain Future

C havez has often said that he would like to remain in power till 2021. Assuming that he serves as president until then, what can the world expect?

As long as the demand for oil remains high and the supplies limited, Chavez can continue to finance and expand his self-styled revolution. He can also continue in his apparent effort to turn Venezuela from a capitalist to a totally socialist society. Economist Orlando Ochoa has predicted that Venezuela's free market economy will eventually be replaced by socialist model with the state having immense control over the private sector. "The state will regulate prices and profits in the private sector," Ochoa said.

Independent analyst Albert Garrido thinks that Venezuela's private health care and private education systems will be the first sectors to come under complete government control under Chavez. "Private health care and private education will be the first in line to be scrapped by the government as part of it's drive toward socialism," Garrido predicted. "The whole country will be geared towards the motto: one leader—one party—one ideology." In April of 2007, Chavez commented that the health care system in Venezuela would have to reform itself or it would be necessary for his government to take it over.

There's been speculation that Chavez's supporters, called Chavistas, will form one large pro-Chavez political party. Currently, he has the support of several parties and each party has it own leaders and structure. The formation of one party would be a consolidation of Chavez's power.

In a speech given in December 2006, Chavez ended the speculation by formally announcing his plan to organize

The words on this mural say, "Chavez, President, on the way to socialism." (*AP Images/Leslie Mazoch*)

all of his supporters into one party to be called the United Socialist Party of Venezuela. Chavez's critics compare the move to how Fidel Castro was able to create a single party in the early 1960s, which went on to completely rule Cuba. Chavez has answered that criticism by saying that the party leaders would be chosen by the party's rank-and-file members and not by him. His critics remain skeptical. "His tireless finger won't stop singling out those who are going to be the bosses," said Theodoro Petkoff, the editor of an anti-Chavez newspaper.

During his presidency, Chavez has created a huge welfare state. In a country of 26 million people, 2 million Venezuelans are now government employees. When he took office there were seventeen government ministries, now there are twenty-seven. Chavez's programs include free university education, subsidized food, and cash benefits for single mothers.

Since his reelection, Chavez has pledged to "deepen" his revolution. He has said that his government will expand health care by building more hospitals and health clinics.

Chavez has also made education a top priority. More schools—from elementary to university level—are expected to be built. There are plans to build as many as fifty new universities.

However, it is clear the schools will not have freedom to teach what they want. Chavez has appointed a commission to create a new nationwide school curriculum that will teach students that "collectivism" is preferable to "individualism."

Chavez's government also increased its control over the press and the television media. In July 2006, the Inter-American Press Association reported that the press in Venezuela was being repressed by a combination of: "restrictive legislation, prosecution of journalists in the courts and harassment of news media." Chavez has stepped up enforcement of *desacato* (insult) laws for criticizing government officials, creating an atmosphere of self-censorship in the media. There has also been an increasing tendency for the government to file libel suits against journalists. Government officials are empowered to suspend broadcasts or revoke the licenses of radio and television stations if they believe the broadcasts are condoning or inciting public disturbances, essentially giving the government free rein to censor the media.

It's expected that even more restrictive laws will be passed to bring the media under tighter control. After a private

Radio Caracas Television, labeled by Chavez as a "coup-plotting television channel," was forced off the air after Chavez refused to renew its broadcast license. *(AP Images/Fernando Llano)*

broadcaster showed a video of energy minister Rafael Ramirez telling oil workers that their jobs would be lost if they didn't support Chavez, Chavez said: "Don't be surprised if I say there are no more concessions to some TV channels."

In late December 2006, Chavez made good on that thinly veiled threat by refusing to renew the broadcasting license of Radio Caracas Television (RCTV). Its license expired in March 2007, and RCTV's tacit approval of the 2002 coup against Chavez cost the station its license. "There will be no new concession for that coup-plotting television channel named Radio Caracas Television," Chavez said.

A couple of weeks after refusing RCTV's license renewal, Chavez announced plans to nationalize Venezuela's telecommunications and electrical companies. The plans were seen as his boldest move so far in transforming Venezuela into a socialist state. "All of those sectors that in an area so important and strategic for all of us as is electricity—all of that which was privatized, let it be nationalized," Chavez said in a televised speech.

In the speech, Chavez also said that he would ask the National Assembly to pass a special law giving him the power to nationalize industries and businesses by presidential decree. That would allow him to greatly expand his ever-increasing powers. Since the National Assembly is solidly controlled by Chavez's supporters, it will probably happen.

"While this is a break with the past, it is consistent with Chavez's drive to concentrate even greater power in his hands and in the hands of his government," said Robert Bottome, who edits and publishes Venezuela's leading business newsletter.

In late January 2007, the National Assembly approved a bill that would allow Chavez to enact laws by decree for the next eighteen months. The measure passed unanimously—Chavez's word will become law. "This process is unstoppable," Venezuelan lawmaker Juan Montenegro Nunez told his colleagues in the National Assembly. "This process is a historic necessity."

Chavez has said that he will seek greater "economic equilibrium" by grabbing more control of Venezuela's natural resources, such as oil and minerals. He wants ongoing oil projects by foreign oil companies to be brought under national

Members of Venezuela's National Assembly cast a unanimous vote to give Chavez the power to enact laws by decree. *(AP Images/Gregorio Marrero)*

ownership. Chavez hasn't said yet if that means complete nationalization or just a change in how they do business. "I'm referring to how international companies have control and power over all those processes of improving the heavy crudes of the Orinoco belt—no—that should become the property of the nation," Chavez said.

Currently, the Venezuelan government has joint ventures partnerships with some of the world's largest private oil companies such as Exxon, Chevron, BP, Mobil, and ConocoPhillips. It's not known if Venezuela is going to compensate foreign investors for their holdings or simply seize them. During smaller-scale takeovers of farms and a tomato processing plant, Chavez has worked out negotiated settlements with the owners.

A recent article by *New York Times* reporter Simon Romero analyzed Chavez's latest power grab by noting: "Though Mr. Chavez steadily adopted more strident rhetoric, he let most of Venezuela's private companies operate unfettered as long as they did not actively engage in politics. But with his re-election in December, Mr. Chavez seems determined to use the momentum—and margin—of his victory to solidify his power and deepen his socialist policies in ways that are increasingly unnerving his opponents."

It's also expected that the government will seize more private property by citing a land law passed in 2003 giving Chavez sweeping new powers to seize property the government deems to be "idle, misused, illegally acquired, or not contributing to social goals." The law also gave the government wide discretion in applying those criteria.

Around 4 million acres have been earmarked for seizure and redistribution to establish farm cooperatives. The law helps Chavez go forward with his goal of moving Venezuela's poor out of cities and onto small farms. Chavez's opponents have denounced it as a political move to bolster Chavez's support among Venezuela's poor.

Relations between the United States and Venezuela will probably be unchanged, at least in the near future. Two days after Chavez's reelection, a top American diplomat said the U.S. was willing to seek improved relations, but Chavez continued to refer to President George W. Bush as "the devil." "I'm ready to talk," Chavez said. "But if you're going to talk to the devil, you have to have strong morals because the devil has many ways to tempt you."

In spite of Chavez's fiery rhetoric, William Brownfield, U.S. ambassador to Venezuela at the time of his reelection, was convinced that relations would eventually improve. "We've been a partner of Venezuela for two hundred years," Brownfield noted. "This is a partnership that will endure times of stress."

Well into his second term as president, Chavez gave no sign that he had any interest in continuing the two-century partnership between the U.S. and Venezuela. He seems to want to achieve total economic independence from the United States and would like to make China the chief consumer of Venezuelan oil, knowing that could do harm to the U.S. economy.

To say that he is consistently inconsistent is perhaps the best way to sum up the personality and presidency of Hugo Chavez. He fluctuates between being a dreamer and a practical politician. He embraces and praises socialism, but acts like a shrewd capitalist when it comes to making oil deals. There's no question that he truly loves his country, but his drive to be an absolute ruler, a dictator, might prove to be more powerful than his patriotism.

Dr. Edmundo Chirinos, a Venezuelan psychiatrist who says he's known every Venezuelan president since 1958, some even as patients, has offered an insightful description of Chavez: "He is ill-humored and difficult when he feels frustrated," Chirinos said, but went on to say that:

> When least expected, he shows his sense of humor, speaks with familiarity to strangers and friends alike, makes jokes and entertains people. At times he is unjust in his judgments, at other times he is over tolerant. His character is unpredictable and disconcerting. We can know him in depth only if we join the criticism of his adversaries with the idolatry of his followers and strain them through the colander of logic and objectivity. He prefers to embrace dreams that seem impossible to achieve rather than confronting the harsh realities of life.

Having said that, Chirinos then opined, "Except for his power, he is no different than you or me."

Map of Venezuela

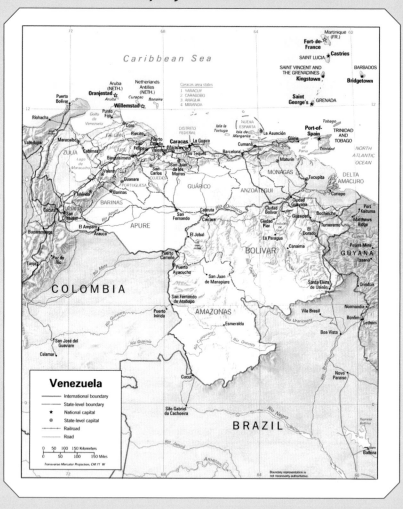

Timeline

1954 Born in Sabaneta, Venezuela, on July 28.

1971 Enrolls in Venezuelan Military Academy.

1975 Graduates from academy; becomes commissioned officer.

1982 Organizes Bolivarian Revolutionary Movement.

1989 Refuses to shoot rioters during riots in Caracas.

1992 Leads failed military coup against Venezuelan government; imprisoned.

1994 Released from prison; resumes political activism.

1998 Elected president of Venezuela.

1999 Persuades Venezuelans to approve new constitution.

2000 Reelected president under new constitution.

2002 Survives military coup.

2004 Wins recall referendum.

2006 Calls U.S. president George W. Bush "the devil" in a speech at United Nations; reelected to another six-year term as president in December.

2007 Preliminary vote of Venezuela's National Assembly gives Chavez power to enact laws by decree.

Sources

CHAPTER ONE: Oil and Baseball

p. 11, "illegitimate president . . . result of a fraud," Greg Palast, "Hugo Chavez," *The Progressive*, July 2006, 37.

p. 12, "the devil . . . peoples of the world," Ian James, "Venezuelan President Calls Bush 'The Devil,'" *Sarasota (Fl.) Herald-Tribune*, September 21, 2006.

p. 19, "Oil is a geopolitical weapon . . ." Nikolas Kozloff, *Hugo Chavez: Oil, Politics and the Challenge to the U.S.* (New York: Palgrave Macmillan, 2006), 7.

p. 15, "They inculcated to us . . ." "Hugo Chavez Interview." *ABCnews.com,* September 16, 2005, http://abcnews.go.com/Nightline/International/ story?id= 1134098&page=1.

p. 15, "one of my greatest dreams . . ." "Hugo Chavez Interview," *ABCnews.com.*

p. 15, "The army for me . . ." Clifford Thompson, editor, *Current Biography Yearbook 2000* (New York: H.W.

Wilson Company, 2000), 105.

p. 22, "Watching him pass . . ." Ibid., 66.

CHAPTER TWO: Young Revolutionary

p. 26, "We did it to prepare . . . " Richard Gott, *In the Shadow of the Liberator: Hugo Chavez and the Transformation of Venezuela* (London: Verso, 2000), 38.

p. 27, "I swear before you . . ." Ibid., 40.

p. 28, "What has been called . . ." Ibid., 40-41.

p. 30, "I was just a simple soldier then . . ." John Lee Anderson, "The Revolutionary," the *New Yorker*, September 10, 2001.

p. 32, "Look here major, is it true . . ." Gott, 49.

CHAPTER THREE: Coming to Power

p. 35, "We had been on the alert . . ." Gott, *In the Shadow of the Liberator*, 68.

p. 35-36, "I can't make it . . . don't send me anything," Ibid., 68

p. 36, "The civilians didn't show up . . ." Ibid., 69.

p. 37, "Comrades: unfortunately, for the moment . . ." Ibid., 70-71.

p. 38, "The first days were like being in a grave . . ." Thompson, *Current Biography Yearbook 2000*, 106.

p. 39-40, "We started studying things . . ." Ibid.

p. 42, "Chavez has become kind of a . . ." Gabriel Escobar, "Venezuelan Ex-Plotter Turns Cult Politician," *Washington Post*, July 24, 1994.

p. 44, "What people hadn't counted on . . ." Diana Jean Schemo, "Venezuelan Pulls Off Revolution at the Polls," *New York Times*, December 9, 1998.

p. 45, "We're witnessing a real revolution . . ." Diana

Jean Schemo, "Renegade Officer Favored in Venezuelan Election Today," *New York Times*, December 6, 1998.

p. 46, "nobody was really sure . . ." Diana Jean Schemo, "Venezuelans Elect An Ex-Coup Leader As Their President," *New York Times*, December 7, 1998.

p. 46, "His statements have ranged . . ." Ibid.

p. 46, "is in the past . . ." Ibid.

p. 46-47, "Mr. Chavez's speeches today are more . . ." "Venezuela's Electoral Revolt," *New York Times*, December 8, 1998.

p. 47, "The only candidate heroic enough . . ." Tim Padgett, "Advice for a President-to-Be: How Venezuela's Hugo Chavez Frias can rule both wisely and well," Time *International*, December 21, 1998, 29.

p. 47, "But the bigger question . . ." Ibid.

CHAPTER FOUR: Consolidating His Power

p. 48, "If you try to assess me . . ." Larry Rother, "Venezuela's New Leader: Democrat or Dictator?" *New York Times*, April 10, 1999.

p. 49, "while Venezuelans overwhelmingly supported radical reform . . ." "Emergence of a Venezuelan Potentate." *New York Times*, August 21, 1999.

p. 51, "There is great talk about democracy . . ." Alma Guillermoprieto, "The New Venezuela," *National Geographic*, April 2006, 101.

p. 51, "In the past . . . " Ibid.

p. 55, "They should shoot me . . . " "Venezuela disaster 'worst this century.'"*BBCNews.com*, December 29, 1999, http://news.bbc.co.uk/2/hi/americas/581579.stm.

p. 56, "what would be the opinion . . ." "Hugo

Chavez," *Contemporary Hispanic Biography Vol. 1*
(Detroit: Thomson Gale, 2002), 45.

CHAPTER FIVE: Coup

p. 57, "Dissident military factions . . ." Richard Gott,
Hugo Chavez and the Bolivarian Revolution (London:
Verso, 2005), 223.

p. 57-58, "To provoke military action . . ." Ibid., 224.

p. 60, "Mr. President, I was loyal . . ." Kozloff, *Hugo
Chavez: Oil, Politics, and the Challenge to the U.S.*, 92.

p. 61, "Save your people and save yourself . . ." Gott, 227.

p. 61-62, "With yesterday's resignation . . ." "Hugo Chavez
Departs," *New York Times*, April 13, 2002.

p. 62, "I told them . . ." Ibid., 229.

p. 62, "I told them that . . ." Ibid.

p. 65, "Then, you are still the president . . ." Ibid., 233.

p. 65, "I don't know, but . . ." Ibid., 234.

p. 66, "violated the Constitution of the Republic . . ."
Gott, 236.

p. 67, "power vacuum," Kozloff, 96.

p. 68, "the Chavez government provoked . . ." Juan
Forero, "The Chavez Victory: A Blow to the
Bush Administration's Strategy in Venezuela," *New
York Times*, August 18, 2004.

p. 68, "undemocratic actions committed or encouraged . . ."
Ibid.

p. 68-69, "Despite the loss of . . ." Gott, 253.

p. 69, "Basically we are all Venezuelans . . ." "Trickle of
Oil Starts Flowing In Venezuela," *New York Times*,
December 29, 2002.

p. 69, "They have perpetrated . . ." Juan Forero,
"Venezuela Votes by Large Margin to Retain Chavez,"

New York Times, August 17, 2004.

p. 69, "There is a clear difference . . . " Ibid.

p. 70, "preliminary results," Forero, "The Chavez Victory: A Blow to the Bush Administration's Strategy in Venezuela."

p. 70, "I would hope that . . ." Ibid.

CHAPTER SIX: International Allies and Enemies

p. 71, "Tonight, the country has . . ." "Bruised but Unbowed," *Economist*, June 10, 2006. 34.

p. 71, "I pray to God . . ." Ibid.

p. 73, "It doesn't cost Chavez a lot . . ." Larry Rother, "Uruguay at Center of Lively U.S.-Venezuela Chess Game," *New York Times*, September 12, 2006.

p. 74, "tremendously dimwitted . . ." Monte Hayes, "Leftist is favored to win presidency of Ecuador," *Sarasota (Fl.) Herald-Tribune*, October 15, 2006.

p. 75, "GO HOME NIXON . . ." Fawn M. Brodie, *Richard Nixon: The Shaping of His Character* (New York: W.W. Norton & Company, 1981), 369.

p. 76, "We can negotiate with the . . ." Simon Romero, "Early Returns Point to a Presidential Runoff in Ecuador," *New York Times*, October 16, 2006.

p. 77, "friend of terrorists, a friend of Chavez . . . " Simon Romero. "Link to Chavez May Have Hurt Ecuadorean Candidate." *New York Times*, October 17, 2006.

p. 78, "We love the American people . . ." Simon Romero, "Leftist Candidate in Ecuador Is Ahead in Vote, Exit Polls Show," *New York Times*, November 27, 2006.

p. 78, "It's nothing personal against Bush . . . " Ibid.

p. 78, In Mexico, you don't have to die . . ." Manuel
Roig-Franzia, "Chavez's Image Becomes Tool for
Attack in Presidential Race," *Sarasota (Fl.)
Herald-Tribune*, June 29, 2006.

p. 78, "The strategy of . . ." Ibid.

p. 80, "In the Chapare there have been . . ." Kozloff,
*Hugo Chavez: Oil, Politics and the Challenge to
the U.S.*,167.

p. 80-81, "If they want to talk . . ." Ibid., 168.

p. 81, "humanitarian aid," Simon Romero, "Bolivia Leader
Lets Venezuela Send Soldiers, Angering Foes," *New
York Times*, January 9, 2007.

p. 82, "Venezuela is traveling . . ." Gott, *In the Shadow of
the Liberator*, 28.

p. 83, "Here we are, as alert as ever . . ." Ibid.

p. 83, "I read a lot of books . . ." Kozloff, 41.

p. 83, "My God, when I get out . . ." Ibid.

p. 84, "Chavez could say . . ." Alexandra Starr, "Faithful
to Fidel." *Salon.com*, August 8, 2006, http://www.salon.
com/opinion/feature/2006/08/08/chavez_castro/index.html.

p. 84, "not necessarily its most representative figure . . ."
Simon Romero, "Venezuelans Give Chavez a Mandate
to Tighten His Grip," *New York Times*, December 5, 2006.

p. 86, "The speech really hurt his case . . ." Warren
Hoge, "Venezuelan's Diatribe Seen as Fatal to U.N.
Council Bid," *New York Times*, October 25, 2006.

p. 86, "No matter how strong . . ." Albert Aji, "Chavez:
Syria and I will 'build a new world,'" *Miami Herald*,
August 31, 2006.

p. 86, "American imperialism . . .grave of U.S.
imperialism . . ." Ibid.

p. 87 "one-sided policy . . . wild slurs" ""Chavez:

Venezuela, Syria United Against U.S." *NewsMax.com*, August 30, 2006, http://www.newsmax. com/archives/ic/2006/8/30/104644.shtml.

p. 87, "We will back Iran . . ." "With Friends Like These," *Economist*, September 2, 2006, 38.

p. 87, "I feel I have met a brother . . . " "Venezuela's Chavez, Iran's Ahmadinejad Pledge Mutual Support," *FOXNews.com*, July 29, 2006, http://www.foxnews. com/story/0,2933,206204,00.html.

CHAPTER SEVEN: Destroying the Opposition

p. 89, "drunks fighting over an empty bottle." "Damned Whatever They Do," *The Economist*, July 22, 2006, 38.

p. 90, "I will be the president . . ." "Venezuelan Opposition Names Candidate to Face Chavez," *St. Petersburg (Fl.) Times*, August 10, 2006.

p. 90, "I am the candidate of the revolution . . ." *Charlotte (Fl.) Sun*, August 13, 2006.

p. 91, "We differ in that I'd exchange . . ." Simon Romero, "A Venezuelan Comedian Hopes to Unseat Chavez," *New York Times*, August 14, 2006.

p. 91, "I have a vision for . . ." "Venezuela: Comedian Quits Presidential Race," *New York Times*, November 16, 2006.

p. 93, "We're living in a period of . . ." Simon Romero, "Venezuelans Square Off Over Race, Oil, and a Populist Political Slogan." *New York Times*, November 12, 2006.

p. 93, "For all of Chavez's faults . . ." Simon Romero, "Chavez Rides Wave of Venezuela's Oil-Powered Wealth," *Sarasota (Fl.) Herald-Tribune*, December 3, 2006.

p. 94, "the fastest-growing economy . . ." Ibid.

p. 94, "Chavez has shielded himself . . ." Simon
Romero, "Venezuela in Crime Boom on Election Eve,"
Sarasota (Fl.) Herald-Tribune, December 2, 2006.

p. 95, "Mr. Chavez has some powerful advantages . . ."
"The Chavez Machine Rolls On," *Economist*, December
2, 2006. 41.

p. 95, "We recognize that today . . ." Christopher
Toothaker, "Re-election Win Emboldens Chavez
Agenda." *ABCNews.com*, December 4, 2006,http://
abcnews.go.com/International/wireStory?id=2698141.

p. 95, "Long live the revolution . . ." Ibid.

p. 95-96, "It's another defeat for the devil . . ." "Chavez:
New 'defeat for the devil.'" *CNN.com*, December 4, 2006,
http://edition.cnn.com/2006/WORLD/americas/12/04/
venezuela.election.

p. 96-97, "The Kingdom of Christ . . ." Steven Dudley,
"Chavez Puts Religion Into His Revolution," *Miami
Herald*, December 6, 2006.

p. 97, "Christian or Catholic," Ibid.

p. 97, "He's religious in the way . . ." Ibid.

p. 98, "The president's power looks limitless . . ."
"Chavez Victorious," *Economist*, December 9, 2006, 44.

CHAPTER EIGHT: Uncertain Future

p. 99, "The state will regulate . . ." Greg Morsbach,
"What Comes Next for Venezuela?" *BBCnews.com*,
December 6, 2006, http://news.bbc.co.uk/2/hi/
americas/6212430.stm.

p. 99-100, "Private health care and private education . . ."
Ibid.

p. 101, "His tireless finger won't stop . . ." Simon

Romero, "Chavez Plans One Big Venezuela Leftist Party, Led by Him," *New York Times*, January 4, 2006.

p. 101-102, "restrictive legislation, prosecution of journalists . . ." Eric Green, "Sharp Deterioration in Press Freedom Reported in Venezuela." *Usinfo.state.gov*, July 20, 2006, http://usinfo.state.gov/xarchives/display.html?p=washfile english&y=2006&m=July&x=200607201147001xeneerg0. 3363916 (accessed 2006).

p. 103, "Don't be surprised if . . ." Simon Romero, "Killings and Threats Battle Journalists in Venezuela," *New York Times*, November 19, 2006.

p. 103, "There will be no new concession . . ." "Venezuela: Chavez Won't Renew TV Station's License," *New York Times*, December 29, 2006.

p. 103, "All of those sectors . . ." Ian James, "Chavez to Take Telecom, Electrical Companies," *Sarasota (Fl.) Herald-Tribune*, January 9, 2007.

p. 103, "While this is a break with the past . . ." Simon Romero, "Chavez Moves to Nationalize Two Industries," *New York Times*, January 9, 2007.

p. 104, "This process is unstoppable . . ." "Law Would Let Chavez Make Laws by Decree," *Sarasota (Fl.) Herald-Tribune*, January 19, 2007.

p. 105, "I'm referring to how . . ." James, "Chavez to Take Telecom, Electrical Companies."

p. 105, "Though Mr. Chavez has steadily adopted . . ." Romero, "Chavez Moves to Nationalize Two Industries."

p. 105, "deemed idle, misused, illegally acquired . . ." Chris Kraul, "Redistribution Policy Brings Chaos to Venezuelan Land Laws," *Sarasota (Fl.) Herald-Tribune*, September 3, 2006.

p. 106, "I'm ready to talk . . ." Dudley, "Chavez Put

Religion into His Revolution."

p. 106, "We've been a partner . . ." Simon Romero, "Good-Will Ambassador? Venezuela Is Leery of U.S. Envoy," *New York Times*, October 28, 2006.

p. 107, "He is ill-humored . . ." Jon Lee Anderson, "The Revolutionary."

p. 107, "Except for his power . . ." Ibid.

Bibliography

Aji, Albert. "Chavez: Syria and I will 'build a new world.'" *Miami Herald*, August 31, 2006.

Anderson, John Lee. "The Revolutionary." *New Yorker*, September 10, 2001.

"Bruised but Unbowed." *Economist*, June 10, 2006.

"Chavez: New 'defeat for the devil.'" *CNN.com*, December 4, 2006,http://edition.cnn.com/2006/WORLD/americas/12/04/venezuela.election.

"Chavez: Venezuela, Syria United Against U.S." *NewsMax.com*, August 30, 2006,

http://www.newsmax.com/archives/ic/2006/8/30/104644.shtml.

"Chavez Victorious," *Economist*, December 9, 2006.

"Damned Whatever They Do." *Economist*, July 22, 2006.

Dudley, Steven. "Chavez Puts Religion Into His Revolution." *Miami Herald*, December 6, 2006.

Ellison, Katherine. "Venezuela Steers A New Course." *Smithsonian*, January 2006.

"Emergence of a Venezuelan Potentate." *New York Times*, August 21, 1999.

Escobar, Gabriel. "Venezuelan Ex-Plotter Turns Cult Politician." *Washington Post*, July 24, 1994.

Forero, Juan. "The Chavez Victory: A Blow to the Bush Administration's Strategy in Venezuela." *New York Times*, August 18, 2004.

"Good-Will Ambassador? Venezuela Is Leery of U.S. Envoy." *New York Times*, October 28, 2006.

Gott, Richard. *Hugo Chavez and the Bolivarian Revolution.* London: Verso, 2005.

————. *In the Shadow of the Liberator: HugoChavez and the Transformation of Venezuela.* London: Verso, 2000.

Green, Eric. "Sharp Deterioration in Press Freedom Reported in Venezuela." *Usinfo.state.gov*, July 20, 2006, http://usinfo.state.gov/xarchives/display.html?p=washfile-english&y=2006&m=July&x=200607201147001xeneerg0.33 63916.

Guillermoprieto, Alma. "The New Venezuela." *National Geographic,* April 2006.

Hayes, Monte. "Leftist is favored to win presidency of Ecuador." *Sarasota (Fl.) Herald-Tribune*, October 15, 2006.

Hoge, Warren. "Venezuelan's Diatribe Seen as Fatal to U.N. Council Bid." *New York Times*, October 25, 2006.

"Hugo Chavez." *Contemporary Hispanic Biography Vol. 1.* Detroit: Thomson Gale, 2002.

"Hugo Chavez Departs." *New York Times*, April 13, 2002.

"Hugo Chavez Interview." *ABCnews.com,* September 16, 2005, http://abcnews.go.com/Nightline/International/story?id=1134098&page=1.

James, Ian. "Chavez to Take Telecom, Electrical Companies." *Sarasota (Fl.) Herald-Tribune*, January 9, 2007.

————. "Venezuelan President Calls Bush 'The Devil.'" *Sarasota (Fl.) Herald-Tribune*, September 21, 2006.

Kozloff, Nikolas. *Hugo Chavez: Oil, Politics and the Challenge to the U.S.* New York: Palgrave Macmillan, 2006.

Kraul, Chris. "Redistribution Policy Brings Chaos to Venezuelan Land Laws." *Sarasota (Fl.) Herald-Tribune*,

September 3, 2006.

"Law Would Let Chavez Make Laws by Decree." *Sarasota (Fl.) Herald-Tribune*, January 19, 2007.

Morsbach, Greg. "What Comes Next for Venezuela?" *BBCnews.com*, December 6, 2006, http://news.bbc.co.uk/2/hi/americas/6212430.stm.

Padgett, Tim. "Advice for a President-to-Be: How Venezuela's Hugo Chavez Frias can rule both wisely and well." Time *International*, December 21, 1998.

Palast, Greg. "Hugo Chavez." *Progressive*, July 2006.

Roig-Franzia, Manuel. "Chavez's Image Becomes Tool for Attack in Presidential Race." *Sarasota (Fl.) Herald-Tribune*, June 29, 2006.

Romero, Simon. "A Venezuelan Comedian Hopes to Unseat Chavez." *New York Times*, August 14, 2006.

———. "Bolivia Leader Lets Venezuela Send Soldiers, Angering Foes." *New York Times*, January 9, 2007.

———. "Chavez Moves to Nationalize Two Industries." *New York Times*, January 9, 2007.

———. "Chavez Plans One Big Venezuela Leftist Party, Led by Him." *New York Times*, January 4, 2006.

———. "Chavez Rides Wave of Venezuela's Oil-Powered Wealth." *Sarasota (Fl.) Herald-Tribune*, December 3, 2006.

———. "Early Returns Point to a Presidential Runoff in Ecuador." *New York Times*, October 16, 2006.

———. "Killings and Threats Battle Journalists in Venezuela." *New York Times*, November 19, 2006.

———. "Leftist Candidate in Ecuador Is Ahead in Vote, Exit Polls Show." *New York Times*, November 27, 2006.

———. "Link to Chavez May Have Hurt Ecuadorean Candidate." *New York Times*, October 17, 2006.

———. "Venezuela in Crime Boom on Election Eve."

Sarasota (Fl.) Herald-Tribune, December 2, 2006.

———. "Venezuelans Give Chavez a Mandate to Tighten His Grip." *New York Times*, December 5, 2006.

———. "Venezuelans Square Off Over Race, Oil, and a Populist Political Slogan." *New York Times*, November 12, 2006.

Rother, Larry. "Uruguay at Center of Lively U.S.-Venezuela Chess Game." *New York Times*, September 12, 2006.

———. "Venezuela's New Leader: Democrat or Dictator?" *New York Times*, April 10, 1999.

Schemo, Diana Jean. "Renegade Officer Favored in Venezuelan Election Today." *New York Times*, December 6, 1998.

———. "Venezuelans Elect An Ex-Coup Leader As Their President." *New York Times*, December 7, 1998.

———. "Venezuelan Pulls Off Revolution at the Polls." *New York Times*, December 9, 1998.

Starr, Alexandra. "Faithful to Fidel." *Salon.com*, August 8, 2006, http://www.salon.com/opinion/feature/2006/08/08/chavez_castro/index.html.

"The Chavez Machine Rolls On." *Economist*, December 2, 2006.

Thompson, Clifford, editor. *Current Biography Yearbook 2000*. New York: H.W. Wilson Company, 2000.

Toothaker, Christopher. "Re-election Win Emboldens Chavez Agenda." *ABCNews.com*, December 4, 2006, http://abcnews.go.com/InternationalwireStory?id=2698141.

"Trickle of Oil Starts Flowing In Venezuela." *New York Times*, December 29, 2002.

"Venezuela: Chavez Won't Renew TV Station's License." *New York Times*, December 29, 2006.

"Venezuela: Comedian Quits Presidential Race." *New York Times*, November 16, 2006.

"Venezuela disaster 'worst this century.'"*BBCNews.com*, December 29, 1999, http://news.bbc.co.uk/2/hi/ americas/581579.stm.

"Venezuela Votes by Large Margin to Retain Chavez." *New York Times*, August 17, 2004.

"Venezuelan Opposition Names Candidate to Face Chavez." *St. Petersburg (Fl.) Times*, August 10, 2006.

"Venezuela's Chavez, Iran's Ahmadinejad Pledge Mutual Support." *FOXNews.com*, July 29, 2006, http:// www.foxnews.com/story/0,2933,206204,00.html.

"Venezuela's Electoral Revolt." *New York Times*, December 8, 1998.

"With Friends Like These." *Economist*, September 2, 2006.

Web sites

http://news.bbc.co.uk/1/hi/world/americas/1925236.stm
For some of the most up-to-date information on Hugo Chavez
and what's happening in Venezuela, visit this Web site of the
British Broadcast Corporation.

http://www.venezuela.gov.ve
If you can read Spanish, this official site of the Venezuelan
government provides information on all aspects of the country,
its people, and Hugo Chavez.

http://www.theatlantic.com/doc/200605/chavez
In a four-page article featured in the online edition of the *Atlantic
Monthly*, writer Franklin Foer gives readers some valuable
insight into "The Talented Mr. Chavez," who is described as
"A Castro-loving, Bolivar-worshipping, onetime baseball-player
wannabe."

Index